DEFYING THE TIDE

An Account of Authentic Compassion During the Holocaust

Written by
REHA and AL SOKOLOW

gefen גפן
publishing house בית הוצאה לאור
JERUSALEM ◆ NEW YORK Est. 1981

The chapters in Maria's voice were the result of Reha's interviews of Maria
in Berlin in 1998

Cover Design and Typesetting: Benjie Herskowitz, Etc. Studios

ISBN: 978-965-229-642-9

1 3 5 7 9 8 6 4 2

Gefen Publishing House Ltd.
6 Hatzvi Street
Jerusalem 94386, Israel
972-2-538-0247
orders@gefenpublishing.com

Gefen Books
11 Edison Place
Springfield, NJ 07081
516-593-1234
orders@gefenpublishing.com

www.gefenpublishing.com

Printed in Israel

Send for our free catalog

Library of Congress Cataloging-in-Publication Data

Sokolow, Reha, author.
   Defying the tide : an account of authentic compassion during the
   Holocaust / written by Reha and Al Sokolow.
      pages cm
   ISBN 978-965-229-642-9
   1. Abraham, Ruth Fromm, 1913-2003. 2. Nickel, Maria. 3.
   Holocaust survivors—Germany—Berlin. I. Sokolow, Al, author.
   II. Title.
   DS134.42.A27A3 2013
   940.53'18092—dc23
   [B]
                          2013026275

"In memory of my beloved husband, Walter,
My parents, Meyer and Frieda Fromm,
Walter's parents, Julius and Elsa Abraham,
And Maria and Willi Nickel.

And in memory of all my brethren
Who perished in the Holocaust."

Ruth Abraham (1913-2003)

In memory of our beloved parents,
Walter and Ruth Abraham.

May their memory be a blessing.

Reha and Al Sokolow

Acknowledgments

We wish to acknowledge the tremendous assistance and support of the following people without whose help and constant encouragement this work would not have come to fruition.

Debra Galant, journalist and producer of radio documentaries, who spent untold hours interviewing Ruth Abraham and getting the essence of her story onto paper.

Marion A. Kaplan, Professor of History at New York University, graciously gave us of her valuable time and expertise on life in Berlin. Besides reading the manuscript from cover to cover, and returning it to us with copious notes on every page, she was extremely involved and helpful in authenticating dates, places and events in Berlin, Germany. In addition to all this, Marion assumed the role of "senior advisor" to the entire project.

Irene Miller, professional translator and researcher, translated the German documents and letters, and with her first hand knowledge of Berlin, Germany, was of great assistance. Her ongoing interest in this manuscript was energizing.

Joachim Nickel, Maria's son, was able to fill in many of the blanks in his mother's story. He gave unstintingly of his time and memory to make his parents' visage come alive.

Barbara Sofer, author and journalist, who, in addition to reading and reviewing our efforts, and spreading the story of Maria to millions of readers via *Woman's Day Magazine*, *Hadassah*, and in *The Jerusalem Post*, was also our mentor and guide in helping us complete the manuscript.

Our niece, Judy Sokolow, and our children, Mark and Rena Sokolow, our harshest critics, were unfailingly there to read, suggest and offer encouragement every step of the way.

We would also like to indicate that the following resources were of great assistance in the development of our manuscript: *Between Dignity and Despair – Jewish Life in Nazi Germany* by Marion A. Kaplan; *The Holocaust* by Martin Gilbert; *The Last Jews in Berlin* by Leonard Gross.

Reha and Al Sokolow

Contents

Prologue

My mother, Ruth Abraham, 87, needed heart bypass surgery, but all she could talk about was the big party she wanted to make 4,000 miles away in Berlin, Germany. Her friend Maria was turning 90, and Mom was insisting not only on making the trip, but bringing her children, grandchildren, and great-grandchildren from the United States to celebrate.

Soon after she came out of the anesthesia, Ruth's first words were, "Now we can have the party."

So, on a cool spring day in May 2000, we all found ourselves in the lobby of the Berlin Hilton. Mom was sitting straight as always, her slender figure, in a wool tweed suit, was taut in anticipation, her hands were pressed together, and her clear blue eyes fixed on the door. At last, the wide glass door swung open, and a round-faced woman with a twinkle in her hazel eyes, and white hair tucked around her face, walked in on her son's arm. Ruth gripped her walking stick and lurched towards her. Then, their arms were around each other, and there was no need for canes. Their cheeks were wet.

When Ruth could finally speak, she turned to her family and said, "This is Maria, our angel. If it weren't for her, none of us would be alive."

I knew, but others did not know.

The full story had never been told. Now is the time.

Chapter 1

The Eyes of Innocence

Who knows why a few survive and many die? I feel that I was chosen to carry on to tell my story. And yet, it makes no sense to me that my parents, my sister Ella and her family, aunts, uncles, and all my other relatives were killed.

To survive, I had to fight, to break rules. I started by taking little risks, but the risks grew bigger and bigger until finally my life was like something out of a movie thriller, fear always with me and my heart always pounding. I discovered that you never really know how strong the will to survive is. But it is strong, stronger sometimes than even an entire army of Hitler's men.

Life is so precious that you do what you must to survive. There is no rule that cannot be broken in order to save a life. A Jew could go to church and pretend not to be Jewish. You could change your appearance, dye your hair, have your nose operated on.

People did all these things. To save your life, almost everything is allowed by Jewish law. The only thing you had to be very careful about was not to get people into trouble who had risked their lives to save yours.

I broke Jewish laws and German laws. I passed as a Gentile and I survived. But none of this would have helped if I hadn't been blessed with a miracle.

Nothing in my childhood could have prepared me for such a trial, such a life.

I was born in 1913 in the town of Löbau, West Prussia, which started out as part of Germany, but later became part of Poland.

My mother, Henrietta, died when I was ten months old. I was told that she was a special woman, and I know her only from the stories of her good deeds. I was spoiled because I was the youngest, and everyone felt bad for me because my mother had died. Every Friday, when my mother baked challahs for our big Shabbos dinner, she would bake extra loaves and take them to the poor house. She was also very beautiful, and my father often asked her to come to his grocery store so that people would come and look at her and then buy their groceries. When she died, after an appendix operation, her coffin was carried through the streets on a horse and wagon, and people from the poor house lined up to watch the procession – she was so beloved.

When I was six, my father, Meyer Fromm, a successful business-man, married my mother's sister, Frieda, who had come to help take care of us.

We grew corn and grains and had a liquor business, and a grocery store where we sold roasted coffee and all kinds of sweets and chocolates. To this day, I can still remember the smell of the coffee and the taste of all those wonderful sweets.

I was the youngest of seven children. My two brothers died before I was born, so we grew up a family of five sisters. We lived in a comfortable house at Kuppner *Strasse* 5, with creeping grapevines, a courtyard garden, and so many bedrooms that none of us had to share a room. Our attic was filled with fishnets, and we had dogs running around the yard. The dogs were always having puppies, and we children played outside all the time.

I had a happy childhood, but my parents were very serious people. To my new mother, lying was the worst thing one could do. She always said, "Everybody is entitled to make mistakes while growing up. But lying – that's out of the question. Because if you lie, then you are capable of a lot of other bad things."

Little did she know that my lying would one day save my life.

In the summer, we would go into the garden and plant flowers and chase the chickens and the geese.

Sometimes, the men who worked for my father would take us out in their boats, and we would watch them fish.

I loved being outdoors, feeling the wind blowing through my long blond hair and the warmth of the sun on my face. My sisters and I would go on long walks in the woods, searching for wild mushrooms. We knew which were the good ones and which would make you sick.

In the fall, we would shake the trees to bring down showers of fruit and nuts. In the winter, my mother would wrap us up in our warmest clothes because it was bitter cold, and we would go sleigh riding with their bells ringing. Sometimes we would go ice skating on the same lake where we fished in the summer.

My favorite day of the week was the *Wochenmarkt*, the market day. The housekeeper would take me there. It was like the farmers' market of today. All the peasants around Löbau would come with their fish and chickens and geese and fruits and vegetables. The marketplace would be filled with the cheerful squawks of animals and the sounds of people haggling over the price of tomorrow night's dinner.

Friday nights were special. The *Grundofen* (stove) would be lit and burn in our kitchen for 24 hours. That was where the cholent for Shabbos would cook all of Friday night and Saturday. There would be fresh challah and always a big festive meal. We usually had guests, as visitors from out of town were always invited. After my father came home from the synagogue, we all sang songs welcoming the Shabbos. On the Shabbos day, we would dress in our best clothing to go to synagogue.

I remember the holidays, like Chanukah, when we were given sweets and small tops, or dreidels, and a few little presents. I remember Yom Kippur, when one big candle, placed in a pot of sand, burned for 24 hours in our house. Yom Kippur began in the evening with the *"Kol Nidre"* prayer. We fasted the entire 24 hours and prayed for God's forgiveness for our sins, and to be entered into the Book of Life. When Yom Kippur started, my father would take off his leather shoes and wear his cloth slippers, as it is forbidden to wear any leather shoes on the Day of Atonement. For us children, it was a privilege to help him remove his shoes and put on his slippers. It was a special honor, and each year I hoped I would be the lucky one to be chosen for this special task.

We lived, Jews and Christians, in the same town, and we all got along. There was no disrespect, no hatred or fear then. We went to public school with all the children of the town. We also had to go on Saturdays, as that was the law in Löbau, but we were excused from taking pens and from writing.

In the winter holiday season, we liked to see our neighbors in their Christmas outfits. In those days, the Christian children built little boxes and put candles inside, and went from door to door to collect Christmas sweets or presents or coins from their neighbors. We respected their celebration of the holiday and enjoyed watching them.

But when I turned six, in 1919, things began to change. Löbau became part of Poland. In those days, it was the Poles – not the Germans – who were more known for being anti-Semitic. Little by little, my family and I began to feel threatened and afraid.

One day, I saw for the first time – on a bench near my school – a swastika, the *Hakenkreuz*, along with the words *"Juden, Juden, Juden."* We didn't know what this swastika was, what it meant or even the name for it, but the words "Juden, Juden, Juden" were known to us and seemed to scream at us. Frightened, I ran home, not knowing what to make of this. There was hatred in those words, clear for even someone as young as I to feel. Then, as more Polish people came into town, strange things began to happen. Polish people would scream at us: *"Geht nach Palestina!"* (Go to Palestine).

These were strange and troubling times. But still, I lived the innocent life of a child, going to school, playing with the family dogs, and sewing little dresses for my dolls. Life went on. But some things, even then, tore at my heart, and some things I can never forget.

One time, when Löbau had become part of Poland, some Polish soldiers came through town. They decided to take whatever they wanted. I happened to be standing in front of my house, across the road from the stalls, and I watched as they entered our barn and took some of our horses. We had beautiful horses that I loved. They were gray and white and big. We used them for work and for travel when they were hitched to our carriage. Our horses did not want to go with them, and there was a terrible struggle between the horses and the Polish soldiers, with the whinnying of the horses and the soldiers barking their commands. The horses tried to turn around, to go back to their barns with their warmth and hay, but the Polish soldiers whipped them without mercy until the poor horses could no longer fight.

Finally, the horses bowed their heads and sadly followed the soldiers away from their barn. This was my first witnessing of cruelty.

I will always remember the whinnying and the submission of those beautiful animals.

Chapter 2

The Winds of Change

Jews were beginning to be concerned about the present and the future. We heard about Jews leaving Löbau, some had gone to America. We didn't know any of these people personally, but it was always a big event whenever anybody in Löbau received a package from a relative in the United States. Everyone would gather around to see. One time, somebody received a package of shoes from America. How fashionable! Like nothing we had ever seen in Löbau.

It would have been easy for us to go to America in those days. Our problem was that we were too comfortable in Europe. My mother would ask, "What would we do there? Where would we stay? How would we make a living?" My parents felt that they were too old to make such a big move, to learn a new language: they were too afraid of starting from the beginning. Aside from that, we had no one in America waiting for us.

When Löbau became part of Poland, we were given a choice: to stay in Löbau and become Polish citizens, or to move back within German territory and remain Germans. We chose to remain German citizens. After all, I had grown up singing the national anthem, "*Deutschland, Deutschland, über Alles*" (Germany, Germany, above all else), and I had felt it in my heart. My mother had loved the *Kaiser*

(Emperor); she said that he was good to the Jews. This was a civilized country that had given the world Schiller and Goethe. It would be hard to leave Löbau, where we had such a comfortable life, but the choice between Poland and Germany was an easy one.

So in 1921, when I was eight, we moved to the town of Allenstein in Germany. I was happy to leave Löbau because I no longer felt safe there and thought I would no longer be called "*Judju* (Jew), *Judju*" by people who were once my friends. My parents chose Allenstein because my father's brother, Marcus, who ran a tavern, lived there. My parents didn't sell their property in Löbau, but rented it out to another family. I think they believed that one day they might be able to return to Löbau. After we left, however, the rent stopped coming and my parents could not pursue it. We later learned that the Gestapo had taken over our house for their headquarters when they occupied Löbau during the war. Everything was left behind – our house, our property, and my father's businesses. Nothing was ever sold, and to this day, I don't know what happened to all that we owned.

Allenstein was a metropolis compared to Löbau. It was located just a few miles from Königsberg, a university town where the philosopher Immanuel Kant was born. In the center of Allenstein was a statue of the famous astronomer Copernicus, a meeting place for all the older children and teenagers in town.

At the beginning, when we first moved to Allenstein, times were good and we had no trouble. I would ride my bike with my friends, both Jewish and Gentile, and we would meet for our adventures at the statue of Copernicus. I had fun, especially in the month of May. When the weather was nice, we would all wake up early and take long bike rides into the forest, singing German songs. In the summer, I played tennis at Jacobsberg Park with my friends, and in the winter, I learned how to ice skate. There was also a movie theater in town, where we saw silent pictures – until I was a teenager and the talkies were introduced.

Our house was located in the middle of Allenstein's central shopping district. We had some spare rooms for boarders, and two spaces on the ground floor that we rented out to businesses. One of the stores we rented was to Singer Sewing Machine Company. My father now made his living by managing the property, renting out rooms and leasing the space for the two stores.

I had begun to show an interest in sewing at this time. As a little girl in Löbau, I had sewn clothes for my dolls. Now, I wanted to learn how to make real clothes on a sewing machine. The man who owned the Singer Sewing Machine store in our building would hold sewing classes for people who bought his machines. We had our own Singer too – a manual model that my sisters and I shared. Even though these sewing classes were not for children, I was allowed to stand quietly in the back of the room and watch. I picked up all the knowledge about sewing that I could. Later on, when I was older, I would become an apprentice to Mrs. Keuchel, who was considered to be the best dressmaker in Allenstein.

In those days, my sisters and I received lessons in all the things we would someday need to know in order to run a household. We had a woman who helped with our laundry, and she would take us with her to the Alle River, where we washed and rinsed all the clothes. This was always like a game, stomping around the river in our bare feet, and making sure that the laundry didn't float away. We also learned to put all the family's towels and pillowcases through a big roller, to press them straight, like ironing. This, too, was a lot of fun.

All the girls in my neighborhood went to a special school for girls – the *Luisenschule*. We learned the usual subjects: math, English, French and Latin. I also learned embroidery, which I was good at, and drawing – which I was not so good at – as well as gymnastics.

My sisters and I also spent several hours a week with a Hebrew teacher, who taught us who we are and what makes us different from others. We learned about the *Torah* and the Ten Commandments. As in Löbau, we had to attend school on Saturdays, but were excused from bringing pens and writing.

My best friend in Allenstein was Jutta Salzmann. She is still my friend after all these years. Her father was a prominent doctor, who cared for my sister Edith when she became ill.

As time went by, little by little, things began to change. Friends began to separate from us. They stopped inviting us, their Jewish friends, to their parties; and when we saw them on the tennis courts, they turned away from us, not wanting to have anything to do with us.

At the movie theater, there were now *Wochenschau* – newsreels – before the features, and sometimes these would include pictures of a new German official, Adolf Hitler. Hitler was not yet the *Führer*, but his power and influence were beginning to grow. In the beginning, in these newsreels, he looked a little comical, something like Charlie Chaplin with his short mustache and those quick goose steps. But there was nothing comical in what he had to say about the Jews, and even less in how the German people began to worship him, like a god, almost, or a religion. As time went on, some of the friends with whom I used to ride bikes joined the Hitler Youth. They looked somewhat like boy scouts, with their brown uniforms and kerchiefs, singing their songs of German pride; but these were scouts who were spreading hatred. Eventually, some of the children who had been our friends began openly to say nasty things about Jews: that we smelled bad and didn't wash, that we were the root of everything bad that had ever befallen Germany.

All around us, we heard praise and admiration for everything "Aryan," or pure German. The government began to award prizes to women for giving birth to Aryan children. German women would be honored for having the most beautiful children or for giving Hitler the most Aryan-looking offspring.

Slowly, after 1933, laws were passed restricting Jews in what they could do. One of the first restrictions was that Jews could no longer employ non-Jewish women under the age of 45. We had always had household help, in Löbau and in Allenstein. So, when our housekeeper in Allenstein suddenly quit, it was a shock. Other workers also became reluctant to work for Jews. My father began to find it hard to find tradesmen to come and repair things that broke in our house. Doctors who had been happy to take care of us over the years suddenly didn't want to see us anymore. Even our piano teacher became uncomfortable giving us lessons because we were Jewish. Only my mother's seamstress – who had taken me on as an apprentice – kept up our arrangement. She let me continue working because my mother was such a good customer and because I was always a good worker, reliable and very eager to learn. So, even when times were difficult, I tried to learn all I could about sewing.

As time went on, what was happening in Germany became very clear to us, like handwriting on the wall. The charges against Jews increased, making us feel very threatened and unsure of the future.

From the start, the worst treatment was reserved for Jews who came from Poland. I remember a lovely man, *Herr* Shimborski, whom my father first met in synagogue. He was our shoemaker. After the First World War he had come to Allenstein from Poland, where he had served in the army. He was very successful and beloved in the community, with a big family, and steadily he was making his shoe business bigger and moving up in the world. The problem started when Herr Shimborski wanted to buy some additional property. His few remaining Gentile friends advised him: "We don't want you to get hurt. We can't change the politics here. Don't buy this property. Please leave Germany."

Although he was shocked and hurt at the time to hear this from his friends, Herr Shimborski was actually lucky because of this warning. He listened to what his friends said and was one of the first Jews to get out of Allenstein. First he sent his children to Palestine, then he and his wife followed. Other Jews also began to leave.

I recall my family again speaking about leaving but, tragically, they did not, probably for the same reasons they did not leave for America: "What would we do there? Where would we stay? How would we make a living?"

We all began to feel, even in the late 1920s and early 1930s, uncomfortable within ourselves. Nothing around us seemed safe anymore. Before, when our family went to synagogue on Shabbos or holidays, we would stand outside, chatting with other families. Now, everybody went right home after services because we didn't want to draw attention, to show a group of Jews together, talking and having a pleasant time. Every time we went out in public, for any reason, we watched ourselves carefully. We did not want anybody to be able to point, ever, and say, "Look how the Jews behave." We began to learn how to blend into the background without being noticed, to become almost invisible.

Even as a young girl, I could see and feel the weight of all this resting heavily on my parents' shoulders. I overheard them talking more seriously about the possibility of leaving Germany, of getting visas to other countries. But even as they spoke about it, I knew my parents were half-hearted about leaving Germany. They used the same reasons as before, and they had lived all their lives in Germany. They were afraid to start again in a new country where they would be strangers.

My parents were now concerned about me and about my future, as it was no longer possible for me to continue working for Keuchel as her apprentice. The laws separating Jews from Gentiles forbade her from employing me.

My parents thought I should leave for a bigger place where I would have a chance to continue learning. We decided that I would go to where my three married sisters lived, Berlin.

19

My first memory of Berlin was when I was only nine years old, and we went there for my sister Anna's wedding. In those days, a trip to Berlin was a very special occasion, and it was especially exciting since I was to be part of the wedding. Anna was a very intelligent girl, with great musical talent. My parents had sent her to study piano at a conservatory in Düsseldorf. Her wedding to Julius Aron, a boy from Berlin, was the most elegant thing I had ever seen. My cousins and I all got to wear special white dresses, and for months we practiced our parts as if we were going to perform in a ballet.

At the end, we threw our veils into the air, just as we had been instructed, and – for the briefest moment, one I will always remember – the veils formed the shape of a *Magen David*, a Star of David.

Chapter 3

Branded in Berlin

Berlin was a large, sophisticated city with many Jews. There was culture – art, music, and theater. In Berlin, Jews were able to blend in and not be noticed. We had the freedom to go and do as we pleased – the nightlife, the cabarets. With all the intermarriage between Jews and Gentiles, we would be safe there. Or so we thought.

Most people, when they hear about Berlin in the 1920s and '30s, think about Marlene Dietrich. I saw her in the film *The Blue Angel* when I was still living in Allenstein. But a religious Jewish 17-year-old girl didn't go around immodestly dressed, or smoke cigarettes or go to cabarets. I moved to Berlin without my parents, as they had to remain behind in Allenstein in order to finish up their affairs. I didn't have my own apartment, but since my three sisters, Edith, Anna, and Ella now lived in Berlin, I moved around, staying first with one sister and then another. And I would often go to Allenstein to visit with my parents.

When I think about my first years in Berlin, I remember places like the farmers' market where I would buy fruits and vegetables and meet my sisters. We were always a close family, and I looked forward to all the wonderful meals, with all kinds of fresh food from the market, that were being prepared. I also remember the beautiful stores, passing the display windows, and seeing everything that was at the height of fashion.

But even then, in the early 1930s, there were the first signs of all the evil that was to come.

The first one in my family to really sense it, or at least to do anything about it, was my sister Betty. She was called the "lawyer" of our family because she was outspoken, courageous, and bold. In 1932, she had seen a gang of young thugs beat up some Jews. This affected her very much and she said that she regarded this as a warning for the Jews. I remember her saying, "I cannot live in this country any longer; I'm leaving for a place where I belong." Betty was going to Palestine.

My parents were shocked and horrified. They refused to give Betty either their blessing or their money. Palestine! Arabs, desert, and farmers! No one in our family or any of our friends was interested in becoming a farmer, not even in the Jewish homeland. All the German Jews we knew felt that Germany was their homeland.

And so, Betty left without a proper goodbye. The break-up of our family had begun. Little did we know that this would be just the beginning.

Even though my life in Berlin was not easy-going or glamorous, I did enjoy, in my earliest days there, some of the excitement of living in such a sophisticated place. First of all, my sisters all lived in apartments near Kurfürstandamm, a very long, beautiful street, running from the Gedächtniskirche-Halensee. It was located in a lovely section of town where many Jewish people lived. I would often walk this street and look into the windows of some of the finest shops in all of Europe, and pass the outdoor cafés. My three brothers-in-law were successful businessmen. Since their husbands were prosperous, my sisters were able to lead comfortable lives as housewives who didn't work outside the home. They led a typical middle-class type of life.

My sister Ella loved fresh flowers and had a regular account with her neighborhood florist. Anna's husband, Julius, kept his own boat in the early days and liked every kind of water sport. Their son, Werner, was a fanatic about car racing, always listening to races on

22

the radio. My brother-in-law, Fritz Meyerhoff, Edith's husband, was especially loved by all the small children, because he was funny and kind and loved to play little pranks. He also loved dogs and had a greyhound. It was a fine life in the early days, and sometimes I could not believe that I actually lived in such a splendid place.

One of my guides to all the splendor of Berlin was my mother's brother, my favorite uncle, Max Lewin, an executive for a cigarette company, who was quite the man about town. He was a connoisseur of all the best that Berlin had to offer in those years. Feeling sorry that we had lost our first mother, Max took us all under his wing. Because he was such an important businessman, he got all kinds of invitations to special events and, when he could, he took us along. In the early years, before things got bad, I went to concerts and operas with him. The most elegant affair I attended at that time was the Press Ball, a black-tie banquet that was held once a year, sponsored by one of Berlin's most well-known newspapers, *8 Uhr Abend Blatt* (The 8 o'clock Evening Paper). Uncle Max's company, Reemtsma, was a big buyer of newspaper advertising, so he got special tickets. Nothing could be more fashionable; it was like a coronation with huge expensive flower arrangements, ladies in long glittery gowns, men in formal dinner jackets, and a band playing popular dance tunes. For all the women, there were special hostess gifts under our seats – beautiful handbags.

In the early 1930s, my Uncle Max, the uncle whom I admired and loved so much, did the unspeakable. He married a beautiful Gentile girl named Käthe, and it threw our family into a state of shock. My mother and my Aunt Bertha sat *shiva* for him, mourning him as though he were dead, which was what some Jews did in those days when a family member married outside the faith. But Käthe had converted to Judaism, and the rabbi told my mother and my aunt to get up and stop mourning. Uncle Max's marriage was a scandal for us. He had taken a giant step outside our tight circle of family and Jewish life. Nevertheless, he remained a devoted uncle to all of us, and we adored him.

Aunt Marta, my mother's younger sister, was one of my favorite aunts. She was tall and beautiful, and always meticulously groomed. She carried herself like a princess. She had such a way about her that she could make small talk with any person, even a stranger sitting on a park bench. I watched Aunt Marta and, since I was interested in sewing and in fashion, I learned everything I could about style by studying her outfits, and finding out where she shopped.

Aunt Marta introduced me to one of her tailors, Mr. Katczchmarak, who sewed dresses for wealthy women, as well as costumes for the theater. He took me on as his apprentice and would become very helpful to me in my early days as a seamstress. Later on, he helped me find connections in the fashion world that would enable me to earn money. Mr. Katczchmarak taught me specialty sewing, such as how to make elegant hats and leather gloves. I could not have learned these things on my own because you needed special materials to make hats and gloves – head forms, and hand forms, and fine expensive felt. Fortunately, I was able to do all these things working at Katczchmarak's shop. He liked me because I was a good worker, fast and talented with my hands. Regrettably, I was only able to work for him for about a year. Any longer could have left him with too many questions to be answered, and could have put both of us in danger.

Aside from missing my parents, I didn't lack for relatives and friends in my new city of Berlin. Aunt Marta had a daughter named Jutta who was a year or two older than I. And as a native of Berlin, she taught me everything about her city. We would ride our bikes all around, to the library, to lectures, or special Jewish performances. Jutta and I would often go to one or another of the lakes that surround Berlin, and there we would sit and talk, like young women have always done, about where we would go and what we would do with our lives, and the men we would eventually fall in love with.

I had some glamorous friends in Berlin, such as Hilde Kaminer, whom I had known only slightly in Allenstein. She had already been married and divorced. She was wealthy, and different from the other young women I knew at the time. She had her own car and boat, and she would often go to the luxurious yacht club at Wannsee. We had some good times together, but Hilde's social circle with fast men and fast women and fast cars was not for me.

My other glamorous friend was an actress named Steffi Hincelmann, who performed in theaters around Berlin in the early days, when I first got there. I recall that by March of 1934, Jewish actors and actresses were forbidden to go on stage. So from then on, Steffi could only work in the *Kulturbund*, which was the Jewish Arts Society. As times grew worse and the fight for survival became ever more demanding, the Kulturbund performances were like a tonic for some people. Things were getting worse, but at the Kulturbund, people could at least escape from their worries and troubles for a while.

But even as I enjoyed living in Berlin, the atmosphere for us was already somber and tense. Adolf Hitler became Chancellor in 1933 and evil was brewing. I saw the brown shirts of the Stormtroops (SA) and Hitler's Protection Squad (SS) with their black shirts all over Berlin. Notices appeared in newspapers informing the public when Hitler would hold his rallies and parades by torchlight. Thousands and thousands of people gathered, and I was among them. I, Ruth Fromm, with my blond hair and blue eyes, who looked more Aryan than the Germans, felt compelled to go and see with my own eyes what the rallies were like. The speeches, the singing, the shouting, the prancing about, were all against the Jews. At first, it was fascinating to watch, almost like a horror film. But then it became real, and I was sickened by it. Never had I been surrounded by such hatred.

Life in Berlin changed rapidly. I felt the horror of seeing the Jewish Star of David painted on shop windows owned by Jews, and Jewish people being beaten on the streets of Berlin. If you were in the synagogue, you would be afraid to leave because sometimes Jews would be attacked on their way home from their prayers. We felt more and more alienated. We were being treated as if we were no longer human.

We didn't know where to turn. We prayed that the leaders of America and England would wake up and see Hitler for what he was, and that would save us. But we were not to be so lucky.

To the outside world, life in Germany must have appeared quite normal. In 1936, the Olympics took place in Berlin. The following year, the Duke of Windsor (formerly King Edward VIII), who had just relinquished his crown, came with Wallis Simpson, his new wife, to visit Hitler. There were pictures of them walking with Hitler, smiling, looking with great interest at the Nazi state. When I saw this, I knew we were doomed.

The most personal part of our lives – with whom we could associate and socialize – came under the new Nuremberg laws. These laws governed and restricted our businesses and our professional lives. We became stateless. Jews were considered enemies of the state and no longer citizens of Germany. Every day, new laws appeared; it was without end. Every day it was something else and we would ask, "Tomorrow, what will be with us?" The Nazis kept taking and taking, step by step, a process which robbed us of all the pleasures and necessities of life. Movies, theaters, concerts, swimming in public pools, sitting on park benches – all were taken away from us. Early on, I was able to use the bus and subway. A few years later, I could use public transportation only if I had a special pass to prove that I was on my way to do forced labor.

The Nazis forbade what they called *Rassenschande*, or "race defilement," which meant that it was against the law for a Jew and a non-Jew to have sexual relations. I heard that when they caught a Gentile who had been with a Jew, the Nazis hung a sign around that person's neck in public, to be humiliated for all to see. That was part of the terror, never knowing when they would just harass you or when they would attack you. Or both.

All over Berlin, ugly racist pictures of Jews appeared on posters and in the Nazi newspaper *Der Stürmer*, convincing the Germans that we were the cause of all their troubles. Some posters made Jews look terrible, with big hooked noses and dark circles under their eyes. Jews were called "vermin," like a public health warning. The posters were everywhere, as were signs stating "No bicycles, gypsies, or Jews allowed."

The Nazis were very efficient and well organized in identifying who were Jews, how many children they had, as well as their addresses and phone numbers. They got all these records from the Jewish organizations in Berlin, and many officials were so afraid of the Nazis that they felt they had to cooperate with them. They even knew which Jews had intermarried. They also had the names of Jews who hadn't been to synagogue in years.

Then, the dreaded official notices started coming, constantly changing our hours for food shopping and curfews. Our hands would tremble with fear as we opened the envelope, and we wondered what restriction would be placed upon us next.

It was becoming more dangerous for my parents to remain in Allenstein. All signs of Jewish life were gone; the synagogue and community house no longer existed. So, in November 1938, my parents decided they had to leave and move to Berlin. It was difficult for them, as they had to apply to the Nazis for travel permits. They also had to register as new residents in Berlin to enable them to find an apartment there. But at that point, it was imperative that my parents leave to be in a safer place. They would be reunited with the entire family at last.

Soon after my parents moved to Berlin, we received a notice stating that all Jews must turn in their valuables to the Nazis: furs, jewelry, gold coins, silverware. The notice told us exactly when and where we were to bring in our valuables. My father, in particular, wanted to do everything by the book. He was a gentle, kind, soft-spoken man, and all this terrified him. So, I helped my parents go from room to room to gather up everything of value. We dared not hide anything, for we all knew that the Nazis could enter our home at any time to search our apartment. My parents thought that it would be far worse to be caught with something valuable than to be forced to give it up if anything had been discovered during a search. This wasn't a time for sentimentality. We had to be realistic and face this; there were no tears for our beautiful possessions. We had already lost far more than our fine jewelry; we had lost our humanity.

We made a pile of all our valuables: necklaces, bracelets, rings, silverware, a silver tea and coffee service, some silver candlesticks – all to be brought to the Nazis. It was strange. It was as if we had a premonition, because long before we received this notice, we had taken our favorite Shabbos candlesticks, the candlesticks that brought joy and light to us every Friday night – a symbol of our family's Judaism – to a Gentile friend for safekeeping. She lived on Kaiserallee in Berlin, and had once offered to help us. We had known her for a few years, and before the Nuremberg laws we had often visited in each other's homes.

My father decided that I would be the one to take our valuables to the Nazis. I was the only child, except for Betty who was in Palestine, without a family of my own. I was the one my parents always turned to for strength and support. My father was too afraid to go. "Ruth," he said, turning them over to me, "bring all this to them as the letter says. And come back with a receipt stamped by the Nazis."

I had different plans, plans that I kept to myself. I knew that one day I would have to save myself and hide from the Nazis. The first spark of defiance entered my mind. I thought it would be very foolish to turn in all our valuables. I did turn most of the valuables over to the Nazis; but telling no one, I held back a handful of gold coins and rings. I was given a stamped receipt, which I gave to my father.

Cautiously, I asked around to find someone who could be trusted with my small precious bundle. I was referred to a Jewish goldsmith in Berlin who smelted gold and could possibly take some of my silver and gold and fashion it into a ring. Secretly, late at night, I went to a cellar where he did his work, and told him what I wanted him to do.

He asked me to leave my coins and rings with him and to return a week later. A week was a long and tense time for me to have to wait, and I worried constantly. I thought to myself, "Perhaps I have made a mistake in trusting this stranger, this goldsmith, with the few valuables I have left in the world." But even more importantly, I had trusted him with the information that I was holding out on the Nazis. What if he were caught? What if he were made to betray Jews who had asked for his help? What if my information was wrong? So many fears. The waiting seemed endless. But in any event, I had no choice; I had to do this.

After that endless week had passed, I hurried back to the goldsmith. To my great relief, he was still there. He had not disappeared. He had made a ring for me with the initial "R". A crude-looking ring, it didn't even look like gold. It looked black, like a dull mixture of copper or granite, like something that had been buried for a long time.

I wore my ring whenever my parents were not around. My father would have gone crazy if he had known I had held back some valuables and had a ring made. He would have been not only scared to death – but furious! He would have said that I was inviting trouble by cheating the Nazis. Still, I had to tell someone, so I told my sisters, all of whom preferred not to know what I had done. But I really became attached to my ring. It was my token of good luck, my symbol of defiance, even courage, as I knew I had taken a great risk and gotten away with it.

All this was the first step; it was a preparation for a very difficult life ahead of me – my life in hiding. I had begun to develop a plan, a way of living among Germans, of blending in. I believed that with my physical features, I could pass as an Aryan. I chose an unfamiliar path to follow and, like everyone else, I did not know what would happen, or where I would eventually end up. The only thing I was sure of was that the more desperate my situation became, the more I wanted to live. Even as a single young woman, I knew that I would do my best to outsmart and defy the Nazis in as many ways as I could.

We were always on the alert: we watched and waited, wondering what would befall us next, but did not know what to do about it. We began to make mental lists of Gentile friends whom we could count on and trust, such as merchants who would defy Hitler's rules and sell things to us that Jews were not supposed to have. When war actually came, food and many other necessities were rationed. This set the stage for the black market where some Jews might be able to make money and perhaps survive. Our survival would depend upon reliable contacts. Every person we knew and met became either an ally or a potential enemy.

How to survive was the constant topic of conversation among Jews. Everyone had a different opinion. In my family, my father was petrified of being found in violation of any of the new laws against the Jews. His strategy was to follow each new regulation to the letter and to pray even more fervently to God. My sisters, Edith and Anna, with their husbands, were exploring options for escape, looking for distant relatives who had relocated in other countries and could provide the necessary paperwork to get a visa.

My sister Ella was too docile to express her own opinion, but her husband, Martin, believed, as many did, that Jews were too valuable to Germany for the Nazis to destroy. He was sure that the Nazis would eventually come to their senses. They would use the Jews to their advantage in order to win the war. And, of course, there were many, like my sister Betty, who felt that the only solution was to go to Palestine. Around Berlin, special meetings were held where young Jewish adults like me went to lectures about life in Palestine, Zionism, and farming.

As for me, to provide for life's necessities wherever I might find myself, I secretly began to put aside, here and there, whatever I could – like the ring – saving what I could for tomorrow. I learned to listen carefully for information. One day I would hear that it was possible to get a visa to Shanghai; the next day I heard about people escaping to Argentina. I daydreamed about riding in a rickshaw or learning Spanish in Buenos Aires.

Of course, I wanted to get married. Although young and pretty, I did not have the luxury of just looking for someone handsome or amusing with whom to pass the time. Jewish men, who just a few years before might have thought about dating Gentile women, also became more interested in their own kind. When I dated, I had to be very practical, thinking, "Does this man have money to help us through rough times, the wit to think fast in an emergency, and connections to bring us, perhaps, to a safe country?"

There was one young man whom I liked and dated. His name was Samuel, a chemist, who had attended the Max Planck Institute. In those days, dating was very innocent, and most of what we did was go on walks around Berlin. Sometimes, we went to lectures about Palestine. There, we met people who called themselves the *Blau Weiss* (blue and white – the colors of the Zionist flag), who seriously planned to get to Palestine, so they taught themselves the basics of agriculture. Sometimes, they would link arms and sing songs filled with longing and hope. One of the songs I still sing to my grandchildren and great-grandchildren is, "We are traveling to Jerusalem; who is coming along?" Eventually, Samuel managed to get papers to go to Argentina, but they were only for himself.

Just around this time, in early 1938, I had a strong desire to go to Palestine to see Betty. My parents graciously offered to pay my way, so I arranged the trip, planning to stop off first in Milan to see my relatives, the Zippels – Aunt Malchen, Uncle Yaakov and all my cousins.

Of course, I was also being sent to scout out possibilities for my family's escape, but there was no doubt that I would return to Germany: the British consulate required a security bond from my father ensuring my departure from Palestine.

However, my parents sent me off to the Promised Land with their blessings, telling me that if I should meet someone there who might be a potential husband and would make me happy, I should remain in Palestine and not return to Germany.

31

Chapter 4

A Glimpse of the Promised Land

My trip to Palestine was set for February 1938. My parents had bought me train tickets, and I shared a compartment with three other passengers. I was filled with anticipation of seeing my sister Betty in Palestine and our relatives in Italy.

My arrival in Milan was like a big family reunion. We all sat and got to know each other again, and enjoyed the delicious feast that my Aunt Malchen had prepared. We shared news of the family. Even though this was a happy gathering, we couldn't ignore what was going on around us. We spoke about Adolf Hitler and what was happening to the Jews in Germany. We had so little time. The next morning, my cousin Harry took me back to the station, where I took a train to Trieste.

From there, I boarded the ship for Palestine. The boat was called *Jerusalem*, which I loved. This was the best type of vacation in the world, to be free from all the restrictions in Germany, to live without fear, and to feel safe. That voyage was one of the happiest experiences in my life.

After twelve days, the ship docked in Haifa, a beautiful city set on a mountain that overlooks the sea. From the start, I fell in love with Palestine, with its orange trees, beautiful flowers, and deep blue sky. When Betty met me at the boat, I cried for joy. We took a bus to

Betty's apartment in Tel Aviv, a few hours away, but the hours flew by like minutes with all our talking. As we looked out the bus windows, Betty would point to this and that, proud of herself, of the Jewish people, of everything. "Look at this," she would say, pointing to something out the window. "This is ours." And of course, I told Betty all the news from home, from Berlin, everything new with our parents and our sisters, and how bad things were getting for us there.

We finally got to Betty's apartment. It was not big, but it was beautiful and modern. She kept it fresh and clean. There were tile floors, and a balcony with a little garden of flowers. The scent of nature was right outside, and I could see the beach and sand dunes that were close by. It was paradise to me. She didn't even have to lock the door. It was only one room, but there were two very nice big couches, one for each of us to sleep on. She was so pleased that she had her own place.

Betty worked for a doctor, named Professor Zondeck, who had taught medicine in Europe and had written many textbooks. She typed up his notes, answered his phones, and sometimes helped out as his nurse.

Now that I was in Palestine, even though this was to be a vacation for me, I decided to make good use of my time. I, too, had to get settled, even for a short period. This was something we were all taught to do from a very young age. "Don't steal the day," my mother used to say. "Don't waste precious time."

Everything seemed to fall into place for me there. I met Betty's friend Gisi Wiener, who had left Czechoslovakia in 1934. Gisi was a seamstress who specialized in sewing undergarments, such as brassieres and corsets. This is intricate work – the cut and fitting are very important. This was how I would spend my days, learning from Gisi as her apprentice. She was considered to be one of the best, so I learned how to fit customers and all the ways of making undergarments properly.

When Betty and I were not working, we enjoyed ourselves. There was so much to do: dancing, concerts, movies, and the beach nearby. One very special time I remember was going with my sister to see Toscanini, the conductor, who performed in a concert. There were thousands of people, many of whom stood outside the huge barn with its doors open, listening to this beautiful music; everyone had to bring his own chair. This was so like Palestine – the best culture but very informal, so unlike Europe.

Another favorite memory is the Passover *seder* I had with Betty and her friends. It was very special, my first seder in Palestine with my sister. After the seder, we went outside and danced in the street, which was filled with people dancing the hora deep into the night. I joined them and felt freedom. No longer was I singled out, despised and deprived because of my religion. I was among my people, and for that brief joyous time, Palestine was my home.

I met many young men in Palestine who seemed to find me attractive. Had I wanted to, dating would not have been a problem. But there was no one special, and in those warm, wonderful evenings, Betty and I spent most of our time with many of our friends, often meeting for coffee at one of the outdoor cafés.

I could not help thinking about how it might be to live here for good, to find a way for my parents to come too. But when Betty and I talked about this, we could not think of any solution. So, I knew that I had to return to Berlin to be with my parents. Even though Betty had already settled in Palestine, she herself had entered the country illegally, so there was not much she could do to bring new immigrants into the country. She could not risk making demands, fearing that perhaps the British would check her out and deport her.

Then one day in March 1938, my carefree, wonderful holiday came to an end. While window shopping in Tel Aviv, I came upon a commotion in the street. People were very upset. Some were crying, others appeared to be in shock. An announcement came over the radio, but I couldn't understand what was being said. It seemed as if something terrible had just happened. I approached someone and asked what was going on.

"Didn't you hear?" came the answer. "Hitler has just taken over Austria."

Hitler had Austria! In one way, it wasn't too much of a surprise. We already knew about anti-Semitism in Austria. Hitler had come from there, after all. But on the other hand, it was hard to imagine Austria's Vienna, beautiful Vienna, now belonging to the Nazis. An extraordinary city, famous for its splendid culture, elegance, music, opera, and the home of Freud – and its citizens now welcomed Hitler.

I was stunned. All the fear and ugliness I had experienced in Germany returned, overshadowing my happiness. "What will happen to my parents?" I thought. "What will happen to our people?"

Over the next few days, people spoke of nothing else, and the news from Austria kept getting worse: Mobs threw rocks through the windows of Jewish businesses, Jewish shopkeepers were beaten up right in front of Austrian policemen, and nobody lifted a finger to stop them. We heard about Jews being dragged from their apartments, forced to do degrading things, such as scrubbing streets and toilets for the Nazis. Jews were jumping from windows, committing suicide. It was horrible.

And this was only the beginning.

We did not yet know anything about concentration camps for Jews, but I now feared for my life, for my parents, and for my entire family. I knew that I would not be staying in Palestine much longer. My parents needed me. My other sisters back in Berlin had children to worry about. They were all searching for ways to leave the country; if an opportunity arose, they would go. I would be the one to stay with my parents and help them. I was glad for Betty, that she had this life, that she was safe in Palestine, but I had to prepare to return and face life in Germany.

During this time, my parents and I wrote to each other, but we could not write of such things as Austria and Hitler. It would have been too dangerous and, besides, the censors would have stopped it anyway.

I left Palestine in June 1938. My parting from Betty was very, very hard for me. We were so close and had shared such wonderful times together. We took a bus again to Haifa. When she brought me to the boat, we cried and hugged each other tightly, not knowing when – or if – we would ever see each other again. When the boat sailed from Haifa, it was as if I had lost something very precious. I was grateful for the time we had had together, but I understood that life must go on.

The journey back to Europe was unlike my journey to Palestine. There was none of the happy anticipation I had felt getting there, but I was looking forward to stopping in Milan again and seeing my relatives. While I was in Palestine, my Aunt Malchen had passed away. My heart was suddenly heavy. For the first time, I saw how life could change from minute to minute, how precious family is, and how I would strive to take nothing for granted.

After spending a few days with my cousins, I left Italy by train. When I reached the German border, the officials boarded the train and checked everyone's passport. One of the German guards looked at mine, squinting his eyes, and then passed it to the other guard. They both looked at it and then at me, back and forth, back and forth. They saw my Aryan features, but on the other hand they saw the letter "J" (for Jew) stamped on my passport. They couldn't believe that it really said "Jude."

"Are you Jewish?" one of the border guards asked me, just to make sure.

There would soon come a time when I would learn to be very careful before I answered a question like that. But I had not yet learned to think that fast. At that point, I couldn't even imagine another answer, even though I already knew in my heart that I was in danger.

"Yes," I said, as my adrenaline surged.

Nevertheless, I expected the official to hand my passport back to me. He didn't. He walked away with it. I ran after him, asking for my passport. His response was, "Go back to your seat. You are not getting it back."

I felt like a big door had been slammed shut in my face. I had been to Palestine. I had tasted freedom. I had learned what it was like to be a Jew in a place where you could live without fear, and dance the hora in the street under a big bright moon. Now I was back, and I was trapped. On the ride back to Berlin, I knew that things had gotten worse.

When I finally got to Edith's apartment, my whole family was waiting for me. I put down my bags, we embraced, but the expressions on their faces were serious.

Edith asked me bluntly, "What do you expect to do now?"

What did I expect? I didn't know. Just a few weeks before, I had been on top of the world. I was 25 years old, full of life and enthusiasm. I knew I looked great with a wonderful suntan. I had many friends. The world belonged to me.

I looked at their faces, sad and stern, and saw that a different life was now before me. The words Edith said next came almost like a shot from a gun. "Ruth," she said, "you are a nothing." I blinked. My heart jumped. I listened carefully.

"We all are nothings. Everybody has to save his own skin."

If somebody else had said this, I might have been able to shake it off. But this was Edith, my smart sister whom I respected, who said what she thought.

In my absence, my sisters and parents had made a decision about my life. They decided that it was time to find me a partner, a husband, because the years ahead were going to be very difficult. Of course, no one knew what lay ahead, but it was clear that it was time for me to settle down.

Edith said, "I have heard about a young man."

Chapter 5

Maria Speaks

I had always wanted to be a secretary, nothing more than that. But the times and the circumstances under which I lived as a young woman made my life take a very different turn. Not in my wildest dreams could I have foreseen the experiences that I would have, and the life that I would lead in the years of turmoil and devastation in Germany before and during the Second World War.

I was born to Karl and Auguste Rehm on May 22, 1910, in Lankwitz, Berlin. My parents had four children, three daughters and a son. My father and mother were decent, hard-working, frugal people. My father was a stonecutter who worked long hours, six days a week. He owned his own business and managed to do all the work by himself, thereby saving money by not hiring workers to help him. My father was also very artistic. He was a sculptor. Using whatever spare time he had, he would create beautiful monuments and figurines for our garden. My mother was always at home, totally occupied with caring for us and doing her household chores.

I understood from a very early age that my parents' lives centered mainly upon their work. There was no time for anything or anyone except the family. They had no friends to speak of. They did not go out visiting, nor were we ever invited anywhere to anyone's house. Looking back, I can see that we lived a very lonely and isolated life. I was always so alone, except for my parents and siblings, and sometimes that was not really enough for me. There was no togetherness; everyone seemed to keep to himself except when we all went to church.

I was raised as a Catholic. My father was at one time religious, and as children we would go to church regularly. We all did well in our studies and finished primary school, after which my parents wanted each of us to go out and work.

As a child, I was very quiet, shy, and withdrawn. I had no one to meet and be with after school, as I had no friends. After spending all day in school, I liked nothing better than to go home and remain there. Actually, I really didn't like to leave the house at all. This turned out to be a problem for me because as I was growing up, I never looked for friendships outside of my family. For some reason, I always felt like an outsider, not knowing how to make friends.

When I finished school, at the age of 13, my parents found a position for me as a housekeeper. I was sent far away to the home of an architect and his family. I hated it. I hated cleaning up after them. But most of all, I was terribly homesick. I stayed with this family for two weeks, and then returned home for a short holiday, crying and begging my parents not to send me back there. Seeing how upset I was, my brother urged my parents to keep me at home. They agreed, and I was very relieved.

Now that I had returned home, my father, who was always very practical, became very concerned about my future and asked what would become of me.

"Since I did get good grades in school," I said, "I would like to work in an office, as a secretary." Much to my surprise, my father agreed to this. So, when I was 13 years old, I started to work at Wertheim's department store in Berlin. I was a *Kassenmädchen*, which means I brought the customers' purchases to the cashier. I was really supposed to be a salesgirl, but I was too shy. So, after several months, I was let go.

Once again, my father was worried, but my mother said she had seen an advertisement for an office worker – like an apprentice – in a print shop. I applied and got the job. I worked there for two-and-a-half years. I learned a lot there. After my apprenticeship, I received a certificate and decided it was time for me to earn some real money.

I went to an employment agency that sent me to Israel Schmidt und Söhne, the largest real estate company in Berlin. I was about 18 when I started working there. It was the best job I ever had. About fifty people worked there; most were Jewish, and many of them became my colleagues. They were very decent and helpful to me, and I grew very close to them. The company paid me well, and I must say that I felt as though I was part of a loving, caring family.

I operated a multigraph machine and worked five days a week, from early morning until five in the afternoon.

Unfortunately, three years later, in September 1930, when I was 21 years old, I was told that I could no longer work for Israel Schmidt und Söhne. My supervisor said it was because of cutbacks in the firm, but it was still very disappointing and difficult for me to leave. I really didn't believe that this could happen to me, especially since I knew my work was very good, and they appeared to be satisfied with me. They even gave me a very good recommendation saying that I was a very willing and eager worker. I knew that my supervisor was very reluctant and unhappy to see me leave. I shook hands with everyone there before I left.

About three years later, many new laws were made to restrict Jews and separate them from non-Jewish people. One time in April 1933, I wanted to go into a tobacco store called Lazer und Wolf, but it was forbidden because of the boycott against all Jewish-owned shops. It was no longer possible for a non-Jew to do business with a Jew. Nazis with guns stood in front of the store and told me I was not allowed to buy anything from Jews. Germans were called

"Aryans." We could no longer work for Jews, and Jews could no longer enter shops owned by Aryans. It was unbearable.

Not being interested in politics and never having read about world events because newspapers were foreign to my parents' way of life, I truly did not understand why the Jews were being treated so badly. However, even I was able to grasp how terribly wrong this was. I couldn't understand why it was that the Jews were so deeply hated. Everyone was talking about the problems with the Jews. It was impossible for me to believe that there were such problems, as my Jewish colleagues had always been so kind to me at work.

All this disturbed me very much. After I had left Israel Schmidt und Söhne I thought a lot about my Jewish co-workers who had been so friendly and decent to me. I was very anxious for them and concerned about what would happen to them.

Of course, I never believed the terrible things I had heard about the Jews. It just wasn't true. I began to despise the political party that was spreading such hatred with its rallies and speeches. They were inciting the people against the Jews. The injustice of it was unbearable, and the question of "why" was always on my mind. What had the Jews done? I knew that they had done nothing to deserve this.

I even spoke to my father about it. At first, he could not believe that our people were acting so inhumanely toward the Jews. He said that the stories that were being spread about the Jews being our enemies were not to be taken seriously or believed. But then, after some months had passed, we spoke again. This time he said that those who belonged to the Nazi party, and those who were hateful to the Jews, were pigs. He finally believed that the stories we'd heard about what Hitler and his Nazis were doing to the Jews were true. It was really happening.

Some months later, I found a new job at a Dutch firm named *Neue Jugend*. This firm published an illustrated newspaper for family and youth. From 1931 to 1935, I worked as a secretary and steno-typist for this company. One of my new responsibilities was that of writing and answering letters. This job was to become a lucky change for me because I met my future husband, Willi Nickel, there. He was a driver for the firm.

Willi was six years older than I. He was a very warm and kind young man who loved music, and at one time even had his own band. He loved to have a good time and liked to vacation in scenic places.

In 1935, a year after we met, we married. We set up our first home in Berlin-Kreuzberg. He was a very good husband to me, a de-cent, stable, and loving man. We loved each other very much.

Chapter 6

Dashed Dreams and Shattered Glass

When I returned from Palestine, my sister Edith suggested that I meet Walter Abraham, a young man whom she had heard about. Curious and interested, I agreed.

We first met in late August 1938 for a drink at an outdoor café on the Kaiserallee. I wore my special good luck ring, and the first thing I noticed about Walter was that he wore a ring too – a ring just like mine. He must have also defied the Nazis! I looked at Walter's ring, he looked at my ring, and we both smiled. It was our first date, so we were too shy to ask questions. But I took it as a good omen. It created an instant spark. We had just met, and already we shared an important secret. Maybe, he would be the one to join me in my fight for survival.

Even though there was not much time for romance, I liked Walter right away. I think I fell in love with him. He was what you call simpatico. It could be that hard times bring people closer faster, and as Jews, at this time, it appeared that we were all destined to share the same fate.

Walter came from a financially comfortable family. He was in the furniture business, which he had learned from his father in Frankenthal, a city near Mannheim, about a ten-hour train ride from

Berlin. Walter had recently moved to Berlin and became a partner in a furniture business called Fechner und Preidel, near Alexanderplatz.

At 32, Walter was very sure of himself and very handsome. I didn't mind at all that he had dark hair, warm hazel eyes, and a strong build. He was a good dresser, stylish but casual. When I saw him in his car, a Cabrilli, I thought he looked very sporty. He was an avid soccer player, and he told me that he had organized a Jewish sports club, the Maccabees and Bar Kochba, with which he had once traveled to France for a soccer match. Everything about him was appealing and attractive, and I was more than interested in him. I think he felt that way about me, too.

After our drink, we walked along the Kaiserallee, a beautiful tree-lined street with grand apartment houses and balconies on the west side of Berlin. I still remember that day we first met. Every year, at that time, I think of it, a very hot day in August with the sun beginning to set.

We walked and talked, getting to know each other. I told him all about my trip to Palestine, how wonderful I felt being in a place where Jews were free. And then we spoke about what was happening to the Jews in Germany, and what might be in store for us in the near future. When I told him about how the Germans had taken my passport from me at the border, it made him grasp how serious the situation had become and how much more serious it would get.

Later I realized that despite his easy-going nature, he already knew how grave things were. He told me that he had wanted to leave Germany two years earlier, in 1936. He had had the money and the connections at the time to buy his own affidavit for America, but his father couldn't bear the thought of his son leaving and going so far away. He said that if Walter left, he would commit suicide. Walter was a devoted son, so he stayed – just like I did.

The next time we met was at Rubinstein's, a kosher fish restaurant. This was a more serious date – a real meal. I looked up and down the menu and then ordered the least expensive thing, a carp's head. Nothing fancy, but being very independent, I planned to pay for my meal myself. When it was time to pay the bill, Walter could not get over it. Other girls he went out with ordered a big dinner with all the trimmings and always expected him to pay! But I insisted on paying. I did not want to take advantage. Walter was very impressed.

By now, we were comfortable enough with each other to talk about our rings, and found that both were made by the same goldsmith. At this, we shared a laugh. I thought perhaps this was another good omen, but it was too early to tell what it would be.

After we had met a few more times, I let Walter know that, to me, time was very precious. I told him that I was not looking for a prolonged friendship, that I was a woman who was looking for a marriage partner. I risked scaring him away, but I also had to tell him what my intentions were. I knew that a handsome and eligible young man like Walter could have plenty of girlfriends, but I had no intention of being just another girlfriend.

I spoke a lot about my family and that I came from an observant Jewish home. Walter told me that his family was not religious and, like his father, he worked in his store on Saturdays, the most important day of the week for shopping. But even a secular family like the Abrahams felt strongly about being Jewish, and they certainly expected Walter to marry a Jewish girl.

In other ways, our temperaments were different. I was always serious, realistic to the point of pessimism, while Walter was lighthearted and fun-loving with a wry sense of humor. He loved to tell jokes and make people laugh. But he adapted to my mood and well understood that we could be destroyed by the German evil around us.

For the next two months, we continued to meet and speak on the phone. But on November 9, 1938, life in Germany took a drastic turn for the worse and Walter, for a short time, faded into the background.

I was staying at Edith's apartment in Berlin, at Düsseldorfer Strasse 34, when the phone rang early that evening. I answered and it was Edith's husband, Fritz, who spoke to me in his most serious voice. "Ruth, Berlin is burning. The synagogue on Fasanenstrasse is burning!"

The terror had come here, raging within our community. For a minute, while Fritz was talking, my mind was spinning. I stood up, trying to see what I could outside the window, only hearing half of Fritz's words. I saw nothing and returned to the phone.

"It is very dangerous," he continued. "Whatever you do, don't leave the apartment!" I couldn't think of what to answer. "You must promise," Fritz said. But before I could even respond, he hung up.

His warnings fell on deaf ears. Berlin was burning: this was shocking, horrible news. I knew I had to go and see this for myself, with my own eyes. I needed to be there and felt that I would be all right, that nothing would happen to me, as I could easily pass as a German.

So, I quickly put on my coat and left, carefully locking the apartment, and walked in the direction of Kurfürstendamm, to the synagogue on Fasanenstrasse. I didn't have to walk very far. In just a few minutes, I was in the middle of everything.

Even from the distance I could see the fires and smell the smoke. I could hear a terrible noise, the breaking and cracking of glass. Everywhere, the fires colored the night sky with bright flashes of orange. And there was a stench, a smell of burning that hung heavily in the air. When I got close, I thought I was in the middle of a horrible dream. This couldn't be real. The synagogue was burning. But even in my worst nightmares, I couldn't imagine what it was that fed the flames, what made them jump so high into the sky. It was everything that was holy to us; our prayer books, our prayer shawls, our sacred Torah scrolls, had been thrown from the synagogue, like rubbish, into big piles in the middle of the street and then lit with fire. All around the bonfires, dancing like at a merry carnival of madness, were the Stormtroopers, the SS, and big important Nazis, with puffed up chests, and youngsters of the Hitler Youth.

Their shirts, which were usually so clean and pressed, were filthy with soot and sweat from the shameful and dirty work they had undertaken. They had wild looks on their faces. They were happy, laughing and shouting, singing horrible songs against the Jews. They seemed drunk – if not from liquor, then from the wild power they got from burning the Torah scrolls. It was clear to me that this was what they had been waiting for. And, when the fires were not strong enough, they found more items with which to feed the flames. Then they took their axes and started to hack at the synagogue, destroying more and more so that the ferocious fires would continue to burn.

When they were through with the prayer shawls and the scrolls, they attacked the Jewish shops. These they could identify because they were already painted with yellow Stars of David and the word "JUDE!" in big angry-looking letters. That we already had gotten used to, as well as seeing the Nazis standing in front of the shops with their arms folded across their chests, blocking the doors so that everyone would be afraid to shop there. But this was a million times worse. Now the Nazis took up their axes and shattered all the windows of these stores. They went inside and smashed the merchandise. They were all over, everywhere, running riot – breaking glass, smashing things, looting, throwing everything they could from windows onto the street.

I was standing near a dry goods store that sold blankets and pillows. These, the Nazis slashed open. That image remains frozen in my memory: goose feathers floating in the sky. The air billowed with smoke until the whole street smelled like a barnyard on fire. Ironically, there was a certain beauty to this, like the fall of an early winter snow, the goose feathers floating slowly, slowly down.

For an instant, I thought of Walter several miles away in another part of Berlin and wondered if the Nazis were also destroying his store, his sofas and fancy pillows, and if the goose feathers were floating there, too.

Then, the Nazis went after our men. Those who happened to come upon this scene and tried to flee, and those who had the misfortune to look Jewish in the eyes of the Nazis were screamed and cursed at. I heard the obscene and blasphemous words hurled against them, and I saw them being shoved and beaten on the streets of Berlin, powerless to defend themselves with no one there to protect them. The local German citizens, if they were not taking part themselves, watched as if they were at a parade. No one that I saw came forward to stop this atrocity. I feared for those poor innocent men and for all the men in my family, and I prayed that they were safe.

For myself, I wasn't afraid. I felt as if I were invisible – no one paid attention to me, nobody bothered me, no one told me to go home. I stood there, frozen like a statue of stone, as if I were nailed to the sidewalk. I couldn't make myself move. And I didn't cry – not until later. I watched, barely believing my eyes. Is this true or is it not true? Could such a thing happen in the twentieth century? Who would believe me? I remember thinking, "Will there ever be a time when I will be able to tell what I have just seen, and will people believe me?"

From here on, it was obvious to me that our troubles would only worsen.

What I witnessed that night, would eventually be known as *Kristalnacht,* the Night of Broken Glass. How I made my way back to Edith's apartment, I don't know, as the brutality of what I had just seen totally overwhelmed me. Looking back at that night, I must have been in shock, too overwhelmed to think of calling my sisters to find out if their husbands were safe. The department store where they were employed, N. Israel, had been attacked, but the damage was not as bad as what I had seen that night.

I thought of Walter and was very worried about him, and I hoped that I would hear from him soon. Every time the phone rang, I jumped, wondering "Is this Walter now?"

Finally, early the next morning, he called. His voice was low. It sounded weak and sad beyond words. He did not sound like the light-hearted, confident young man I had come to know, the happy-go-lucky soccer player and businessman.

"This is Walter Abraham," he began. "Do you remember me?"

Did I remember him! Did I remember the man whom I had thought about every day and who, already, in my mind, was to be my future husband? Did I remember Walter Abraham who wore the special ring and with whom I'd walked on the Kaiserdamm? What a foolish question!

He was calling from his furniture store – his former store. It had been completely destroyed during the night. He had gotten there very early in the morning, and even as he spoke on the phone, he said, the Stormtroopers (SS) were still around, and he was terrified of leaving the store by himself. He was helpless and in shock. He saw no escape without running into the SS. His business was ruined. There was nothing to salvage. He was paralyzed with fear.

He asked if I would do him a favor. Was it possible for me to come and help him leave his store? He thought that perhaps I could get past the SS because I looked German, and maybe we could walk out together. At first, this took me by surprise. What nerve, I thought, for him to ask such a thing of me. We had met only a few times, and we weren't even engaged. But then, this was a person in great need, and I couldn't refuse him.

I agreed to come. It took me about 30 minutes by subway, across town to get to Alexanderplatz, and to find Walter's store. It was like walking through a war zone. All around, businesses had been destroyed. There was shattered glass everywhere. I could hardly walk for all the glass. I went to the address that Walter had given me, and I found the building that had once housed Fechner und Preidel, one of the finest furniture stores in Berlin. There was nothing left. It was like a bomb had exploded there. The furniture was hacked to pieces – firewood. Each room, which had once been decorated with fine china and elegant furnishings, was smashed to bits.

Where in all this mess would I find Walter? I called, "Walter! Walter!" Only silence. Only overturned sofas, shattered lamps, dining room tables hacked to pieces. I almost gave up on finding him. Then finally I spotted him – in the back, in a corner, where the ceiling was still intact. He was crouched on the floor, hiding behind something that was not broken.

But he was broken. He was not the same. I reached him and gently took his hand, like you lead a lamb or a small child. He was in shock. He didn't know how to get out, only that he hoped the Stormtroopers would not see us. Together, we stumbled out of the store. And he was silent, completely silent. Finally, after thanking me for having come to help him, he started mumbling, "My mother, my mother." He was worried about his mother. The first thing he wanted was not food or water or fresh clothes or even to return home. He wanted to see if his mother in Mannheim was safe.

We made our way to a public phone. Miraculously, he somehow got through, but Walter could hardly understand her words for all her crying. I could even hear the sobs from where I stood, a few feet away. She was crying with relief at hearing Walter's voice, overjoyed that he was not harmed, and she cried when she told Walter what had happened on Kristalnacht to her, to his father, and to the Jews of Mannheim.

The Nazis had thrown rocks and rotten eggs at Walter's mother, Elsa. And they had taken Walter's father, Julius, with all the other Jewish men, to a place called Dachau.

"Please, please come," Elsa Abraham begged her son.

She sounded completely lost.

Chapter 7

Miracle at Dachau

Walter, clearly a devoted and caring son, didn't have to think twice about going to see his mother; it was understood. Even though it was dangerous, even though the SS were watching all the train stations, even though they could grab any Jewish man off the street for any reason, he needed to be with his mother. He said he had just enough money in his pocket to buy a train ticket to Mannheim. He said he didn't know when I would see him, or what would happen from here. "You will hear from me" is all he said, and then we parted.

I did hear from Walter. He called a few days later from Cologne. He hadn't reached Mannheim yet; it was too dangerous for him to travel there directly, as the Nazis would suddenly board and raid the trains, looking for Jews. This journey would take him three days, dodging the Nazis by changing trains throughout the trip.

But, he asked, would I do something else for him? He said he would like to send me a check. Would I be able to get to his bank and cash it? That would be a tremendous help to him, he explained.

Without hesitating, I agreed to help him. Soon, Walter's letter with his check, for a large sum, arrived. I went to the bank. Feeling very nervous inside, I nevertheless managed to appear calm, and handed the teller the check. Luckily, I was not asked any questions, and he gave me the money.

I went straight home. Now, what was I going to do with this money? I put it in a safe place and waited. A few days passed, and then another phone call from Walter.

"Did you get the money?" he asked.

"Yes," I replied. "I did. What should I do with it?"

There was a pause. Awkwardly, he said, "I know it is a *chutzpah* (audacity) for me to ask, but would it be possible for you to bring it? Could you come to Mannheim?"

Now I paused. All this time, my parents and Edith were listening to the conversation. At first, my parents thought I was out of my mind, wondering what kind of Jewish girl would go to a man in a strange, faraway city, a man whom she had just recently met, who was not even her fiancé? How would it look? Where was my self-respect?

Not only was it highly improper, but it was incredibly dangerous. They asked all these questions while I was still on the phone with Walter. But my sister, wise Edith, stood up for me. "These are barbaric times," she told my parents. "These are the times when one Jew must help another. Let her go. If she wants to fool around, she could do so here, at ten o'clock in the morning."

And finally, my parents understood how important it was for me to go. I would leave with my parents' blessings.

Still waiting on the phone, Walter was assured that I would come to Mannheim. But, I must admit, it was somewhat calculating; I wasn't being totally selfless. I knew I had a better chance of surviving if I was not alone, if I had a husband. And I wanted Walter.

The day I left, I wore gray-and-white alligator skin shoes, a brown hat, and a brown dress with a white starched collar. I didn't take a suitcase, just a purse where I put the cash for Walter. All I planned to do was deliver Walter's money to him and return home.

The train station in Berlin was filled with soldiers, and I heard everybody talking about the visit of Molotov, Russia's foreign minister, to Berlin, which was taking place that very day. I listened carefully, as it was important to know what was going on; it might affect me in some way. But I also heard more than I wanted to hear. There was laughter from the soldiers about the night of broken glass, of how the Jews "were finally getting what they deserved." Evil hung in the air.

I tried as hard I could to show no fear, to look like an ordinary young woman. I sat in a small tight space on the train, tightly clutching my cash-filled purse. It was like a weighty secret, and I guarded it carefully. I looked straight ahead, not inviting anyone to speak to me, and I spoke to no one.

The train ride lasted all night, and I spent the entire trip sitting awake and tense. The train reached Mannheim early in the morning. When I walked off the train, there was a band playing at the station with the SS (special police) and the SA (paramilitary force) singing a song, the words of which were truly terrifying: *Wenn's Judenblut vom Messer spritzt, dann geht's nochmal so gut.* (As long as Jewish blood spurts from the knife, everything goes doubly well.) I walked past as quickly as I could, thankful not to be noticed.

It was raining, and I had trouble finding the house where Walter was. In Mannheim, the streets had numbers like L-14-5 – or something similar – but I knew from my map that it was not very far from the train station.

Finally, I found the house. I went up the front steps and rang the doorbell. It took a while before anybody answered the door. At last, a young woman came out, and she gave me a look that seemed especially unfriendly, even cold.

"I've come from Berlin," I explained. "I need to talk to *Frau* Abraham and her son."

At this, the young woman became even colder. But she told me to wait, and then turned and walked back into the house.

A few minutes later, Walter and his mother appeared and invited me in. It turned out that they were staying with Walter's cousin, Trude Weil. Inside, I saw about twenty women, all huddled together.

The weather was gloomy. The atmosphere was dreary and somber. The room itself was dark. And then I learned why all these women were together under one roof. Their men had all been taken away to Dachau. Nobody knew what would become of them.

Now I could see why the young woman who answered the door had been so distant and hostile to me, as were the other women in the room. Who could blame them? Every woman in the room had a husband, father, boyfriend, brother, or son who had been pulled off the streets during Kristalnacht in Mannheim and taken to Dachau concentration camp. Every heart in this room had been broken, and in this somber house Walter was the only man. The last thing they needed, I thought, was another woman, a stranger, bringing them her own problems.

Even so, they gave Walter, his mother, and me, a little corner where we could have some privacy. I gave Walter his money. He was so grateful and pleased that I had been successful that his eyes overflowed with tears. But his mother was despondent because her husband had been taken to Dachau.

What to do? We talked and talked, and realized it was hopeless.

I remember saying to Walter, "It makes no sense to talk about what we cannot change. Let me make a suggestion. I will go to Dachau to try to get your father, Julius Abraham, released."

First, they thought I was joking, then they thought I was crazy. Finally, Walter and his mother, Elsa, understood that I was totally serious and determined. I meant it.

They said, "Absolutely not." They would not permit me to put my life in danger again. They wouldn't hear of it.

But I was headstrong, and having recently put myself into dangerous situations, I couldn't stop and go back. I had a strong feeling, an intuition, that I would be successful. I would go.

Late that afternoon of November 16, 1938, Walter and his mother took me to the station to catch the next train to Munich, the city closest to Dachau. They gave me the train fare and two pictures – one of Walter and one of his father.

It was to be another long train ride for me, about eight hours through the night. There I was, alone, frightened, and traveling further and further away from the security of my home and family. I had left Mannheim without a word to my parents and sisters. In addition to my parents saying that I was out of my mind again, they would certainly have forbidden me to go, and I couldn't take that chance.

When I arrived in Munich, it was raining. I asked someone where Dachau was. I was pointed to a bus depot right around the corner. There were many buses, and I easily found the one that was marked "Dachau." I got on the bus and found a seat. Nobody asked me for money. Pretty soon, the bus filled up with people, including many Nazis in uniform. Finally, the door closed, and we were on our way.

In about twenty minutes, we approached the camp and I became very tense. The first thing I noticed, right by the entrance, was an electric wire fence to prevent people from leaving Dachau. This in itself was terrifying. What if I got into Dachau and they kept me there? I tried to look for other exits – in case I would have to escape – but I also remembered that I had to appear calm, like a proper German lady.

When I got off the bus, I was asked why I had come. Most likely, I was taken for the wife or girlfriend of someone who worked there. "I want to see the *Kommandant* (commander)," I stated.

"Do you have an appointment?"

"No."

"It's very difficult to get an appointment with the Kommandant. Come with me. I will announce you."

I was led into a small room where the only things were gray desks and metal chairs. While I waited, I could see from the window the *appel*, the roll call that was taking place behind the barbed wire. This was where the prisoners were made to line up to be counted every day. After a short time passed, the Kommandant entered the room. He was very polite.

"What do you want?" he asked.

"There is an old man, a sick man, named Julius Abraham," I said. "He is here in your camp. He never did anything wrong. I want to bring him back to his family."

Since Dachau is much further from Allenstein than from Berlin, I wanted to impress him with the sincerity of my request, so I lied and said, "I have come all this way from Allenstein, East Prussia."

The Kommandant promised to look into the matter. He scribbled his phone number down on a card and handed it to me. "Call me in three days," he said. Then he quickly turned and walked out of the room.

I was left standing there. The first thing I felt was great relief. At least the Kommandant hadn't laughed in my face or asked me why this old man was any of my business. I was still free! And, just as important, he hadn't automatically said no to my request.

But my relief lasted for only a moment, as there I was, by myself, in a dreadful place where I was a total stranger, without so much as a change of clothes. When I went outside, the rain was coming down even heavier than before. I walked right out of Dachau, through the front gate, but I didn't know where I would go and what I would do with myself, with three days to wait. My shoes and stockings were soaking wet.

Just then, a small car drove out of the gate. The driver was trying to get my attention.

"*Fräulein* (young lady)," said the man in the car, "hop in."

At this point, I thought getting dry was more important than anything in the world, and I wanted human company. What would I do by myself hanging around Dachau for three days? I had no idea. But I was not the kind of young lady who could allow herself to just be picked up, right off the street. I knew the dangers of such things.

I said, "If you're looking for a good time, then you've got the wrong person. Think again, I'm Jewish."

"Don't worry," the man said. "I heard everything. I was in the room next to the Kommandant's. Please get in."

I took a chance and got into the car. What else should I have done – stand there and get soaked for three days? I was surprised to see that he wasn't wearing a uniform, and there was something about him that looked more compassionate than menacing.

He turned to me, suddenly very serious. "What I do here can never be made good," he said. "But I want to help you."

He said his name was Josef Müller. It was a name I would never forget. Josef Müller took me back to Munich. "You're not permitted to go to a hotel here," he said. "You can, if you like, stay all night at my place of business. But you would have to leave early in the morning. Otherwise, I can take you to the Jewish-owned Pension Spier at St. Pauls-Platz."

I chose to stay at Pension Spier.

"But before we go to the pension," Müller said, "I want to show you the notorious beer cellar where it all started, where all the meetings were." This was the very beer hall where Hitler had first started, where he began to make his maniacal speeches. I had, of course, heard about this place for years and read about it in the newspapers, but never did I think that I would ever be invited to go there. But since I was always bold and somewhat curious, I did not turn down this invitation.

"Behave normally," Müller warned me in a hushed voice as he was parking the car. "We will see only SS and SA men. Just act normal so that we will not look suspicious."

The hall we entered was very plain, and people were having fun. It had simple furnishings, just chairs and tables as, I would imagine, in any beer hall in Germany. Big pictures of Hitler and the red, black, and white Nazis flags with the swastika were hanging all over the hall. The room was only filled with men singing, men wearing the feared brown shirts and black shirts. Müller had a beer and when I asked for just a coffee, he laughed. But he insisted on treating me.

It was frightening to be in this beer hall of the Nazis, Hitler's old stomping ground, but I knew that the drunken men in the hall would, of course, take me for a German rather than a Jew.

After an hour, we left that place and Müller drove me to the pension.

When I rang the bell, the woman who answered the door looked startled and frightened when she saw me. But when I asked, "Do you know Josef Müller?" her attitude immediately changed. Whoever this Josef Müller was, he must have been kind to the Jews. Or perhaps it was that whatever he did at Dachau was so awful that he tried to make up for it whenever he was outside the camp. Whatever it was, mentioning his name worked. They had a room for me.

For the next three days, except for going to the farmers' market and occasional walks around the area, I stayed in my room until it was time for me to call the Kommandant.

Finally, the day came. I called the Kommandant. He said, "Go to the Munich train station tonight and look for Julius Abraham."

I went there and saw an old man in a striped prison uniform with his head shaved. He looked lost and confused. I knew from the picture that this was Walter's father. Julius Abraham had never met me, so to assure him that he was safe with me, I showed him the photographs that Walter's mother had given me. But he wouldn't even look at them. He had spent less than two weeks in Dachau, but already he was a broken man.

I knew he was in shock, but still I expected something – a small smile even – for my rescuing him from that awful place. But nothing. No smile. No curiosity. No reaction at all.

I led him to the train platform, which was filled with soldiers. It must have appeared to them that I was a German woman helping an old Jewish prisoner, and this they did not like. They began spitting at me. "Aren't you ashamed to keep company with such scum?"

they hissed. What they would have done or said if they had known that I was Jewish too, I can only shudder to think.

During the long train ride back to Mannheim, Julius Abraham was totally silent. He didn't ask me a single question, not who I was or why I had rescued him. He was in a completely different world.

Our reunion back in Mannheim was bittersweet. One moment, they were happy to see a Jew rescued from Dachau; the next moment, they shed tears for those who remained there.

But Walter was overwhelmed. He and his mother could not believe it. I, myself, couldn't believe it. Our sages say that if you save one life, it is as though you have saved the entire world. I felt then as if I had done something quite miraculous. I had the feeling that Walter would propose marriage to me. I think his mother probably encouraged him to do so. And I was right.

On November 19, 1938, Walter proposed. With his father back home, Walter believed he could now leave Mannheim. We returned to Berlin together, an engaged couple. Now we would fight together.

Before we left Mannheim, I called Josef Müller to thank him for all he had done for me. He had shown me kindness, had given me support and hope by assuring me that if the Kommandant would not release Julius, then he would find a way to help me. He also told me that if I ever needed help again, he would be there for me.

I gave him my address in Berlin.

Chapter 8

Marriage and Mayhem

After Walter and I returned to Berlin, I introduced him to my family as my fiancé. It was a happy time for all of us, even in those dark days. An engagement, a new son-in-law whom everyone was very much taken with, was cause for joy. We spoke about our wedding, agreeing to get married as soon as possible. In other times, there might have been excitement in the planning of a wedding, a great fuss over dresses and bridesmaids and music and food, but the dark cloud that hung over us now was too heavy for such things.

Soon after my engagement, I returned to Allenstein so that I could help my parents finish their move to Berlin. While there, my mother suggested that we go to visit the grave of my first mother in Löbau. Although my German passport was confiscated several months ago, I did manage to get a travel pass to cross the border from Germany to Poland and back.

When we got there, we were shocked to discover that the cemetery had been demolished. There were no stones, no monuments, nothing to mark this sacred ground. Where my mother's grave had once been, a potato field stood.

We were confused, but quickly we grew angry. We walked back into town and went to the magistrate's office, where we made an official complaint. They looked at us as if we were crazy. They probably thought: How dare they complain about something as unimportant as the disappearance of Jewish graves?

There were no longer any Jews left in Löbau, and now there was no cemetery. My mother and I understood that we were completely powerless. We couldn't get out of Löbau fast enough. It was a long, sad train ride back to Allenstein.

Two weeks later, we returned to Berlin. We were preparing for my wedding, which would take place on January 15, 1939, at the only synagogue that had not been destroyed on Kristalnacht. The biggest problem we had was finding a rabbi. During Kristalnacht, most of the rabbis had been taken to concentration camps. Luckily, we were able to find one, Dr. Swarsansky, who had recently been freed from one of the concentration camps. He was one of the few fortunate ones who had been able to prove that he had an affidavit to leave Germany. Once he convinced the Nazis of this, he was released.

Every young woman dreams of what her wedding will be like. My dream was of wearing a long white gown and having my parents escort me to the *chuppa*, the wedding canopy. There would be music and beautiful flowers, and I would be surrounded by all my friends and relatives. This was not to be. From my closet, I chose a plain white street-length summer dress with buttons down to the hem. Carrying a few flowers in my arm and wearing a small white head covering, I was led down the aisle by my parents to where Walter and the rabbi waited.

We had only close family at the wedding: my parents, my sisters and their husbands, Walter's parents, and his grandparents, Ludwig and Clara Strauss, as well as an old family doctor who had known me for many years.

Dr. Swarsansky, still bearing the wounds he suffered at the camp, performed the ceremony. At the end, Walter stomped on a glass in symbolic remembrance of the destruction of the two ancient Temples in Jerusalem, and everyone said *"Mazel tov,"* good luck. Afterwards, we went to a restaurant for the wedding meal. Because we had so few guests, I had to search the streets myself to gather a *minyan* – ten men – so that we could recite the grace after the meal together. For two or three hours, we all managed to put aside the troubles that surrounded us. We were happy, except for Walter's father. Julius was sitting so quietly with his eyes sunken and vacant, looking better than when I'd seen him last, but there was no joy left in him.

Walter and I had no honeymoon, but we spent our first night as newlyweds in a small hotel in Berlin.

As a place to live, we rented a cramped two-bedroom apartment on Düsseldorfer Strasse 44, which we had to share with an elderly Jewish couple. The only good thing about that apartment was that it was close to my sisters and my parents. But it was difficult sharing such a small space with an old couple. It was especially difficult for me because we had to share a kitchen, and the couple did not keep kosher. Walter had not been raised in an Orthodox home, but still it bothered him because he knew how hard it was for me to cook under such conditions. We weren't happy about the apartment, but we tried to make the best of it. We were grateful to have a roof over our heads.

Walter and I were a good team. I was the anxious, worrying type. He had a much more easy-going disposition. I was afraid that if I took it easy and wasn't on guard, something terrible would happen. Walter had this mazel – luck – that always made things turn out all right for him. I was like a cat that could smell danger coming around the corner. But Walter could calm me down and sometimes even make me laugh. He kept my nerves steady. He gave me hope.

For all Jews, the noose tightened. When the war began in 1939, so, too, began the night curfew for Jews.

During this time, more than ever before, every Jew with any money or connections was trying to find a visa to escape from Germany. At least the young Jews were. People like my parents had

62

already given up. My mother had written to a distant cousin in the United States, named Shapiro, asking for an affidavit. There was no response. The rest of the family spent hours traveling to embassies, pleading with officials from other countries, paying for affidavits. Much of this effort was in vain, and many of the papers were false. The borders had closed.

My sisters Edith and Anna managed to get out with their families. Edith and her family had managed to obtain visas to immigrate to Uruguay. On the last day of March 1939, Walter and I took them to Tempelhof Airport to see them off. It was heart-breaking. We were happy for Edith, Fritz, and their son, Henry, of course – happy that they were heading for safety. But we were sad to see them go and afraid that we might never see them again.

After the plane took off, we returned home with heavy hearts. For the next few days, we waited anxiously to hear if they had landed safely and whether they had, in fact, made their escape from Hitler. As it turned out, their visas to Uruguay were no good. But Edith was lucky. She was able to contact a Jewish woman in London whom she had met years earlier. This woman, Mrs. Grozinsky, agreed to sponsor them, and so they were allowed to stay in England as refugees.

Anna's son, Werner, got out next, on a *Kindertransport* – transports of children leaving Germany – to London in the summer of 1939. A synagogue in London sponsored him, and he stayed with two different families for the next nine months, until he was finally able to reunite with his parents. It was very hard sending a 14 year-old boy away on his own; but with the way things were, he had to leave Germany by any means possible. Edith made all the arrangements. She also tried to convince Ella to send her children, Helga and Johnny, on the Kindertransport. But Ella's husband, Martin, refused, insisting that the family stay together.

Anna and her husband, Julius, were the last to leave – but the war had started by then. It was already during the period of

Verdunkelung, the mandatory blackout during the air raids over Berlin. Julius had a second cousin, Mr. Klein, in Philadelphia, who was able to bring over about 40 families from Europe. It cost him a fortune, thousands of dollars for each family. For a while things looked quite shaky for them, as Julius' cousin was beginning to have troubles with the consulate. But in the end, Julius was able to book passage on a Dutch steamship out of Rotterdam, and he and my sister got safely to America where soon after, they were reunited with Werner.

The rest of the family – Walter and I, his parents and grandparents, my sister Ella and her family, and my parents, remained. My Aunt Marta and her husband Sally also remained. Uncle Sally worked for the Jewish community. Little did we know that it would later become his bitter duty to help the Nazis round up Jews for the transports to the concentration camps.

It was hard, even before the war started, to make a living. Walter's store had been destroyed during Kristalnacht, and he was out of work. As newlyweds, we lived off our savings and from the little money I could make with a sewing machine, altering clothes.

Things got worse when the war began. I remember it vividly. I was in a drug store on Kurfürstendamm, when I suddenly noticed a commotion and heard an announcement coming from a radio in the street. At first, I thought it was just more orders and restrictions from the Nazis against Jews, but then I realized it was much more serious.

Germany was at war. I ran out into the street with everyone else. There was Walter, who had planned to meet me inside the store.

No one knew what war would bring. We had hoped there would finally be an end to Hitler. But before that could happen, there would be much suffering: bombs, disappearances, destruction, and food shortages. Now, our only objective was to survive. We had been vigilant before, but now we had entered a stage where we became totally committed to staying alive.

Walter and I tried to leave Germany, but we weren't successful. In 1940 we went to Hamburg to try to find an escape route. By some stroke of luck, we already had a visa to go to Russia. We were hoping for a visa that would let us go from Russia into Shanghai. That had been a popular escape route for a while, but we were now out of luck.

In March of 1941, forced labor began – the drafting of all Jews between the ages of fifteen and sixty-five. We had no choice; we had to obey whatever they demanded, go wherever they sent us. The wages were almost nothing – maybe 12 *Reichsmark* (German currency)a week, on which we had to pay high taxes – but at least we now had work, and with that there was some hope that perhaps the Nazis did need us and would allow us to live.

In September 1941, we were forced to buy and sew a big yellow Star of David, with the word "Jew" written on it, onto all our clothing to make it easy for us to be recognized as Jews.

I already had a plan to use my reversible coat. I sewed the Star on only one side of the coat so when I went to work I was a Jew, and that was the side I showed to the world. But sometimes, I would need to pass as a Gentile. Then, all I had to do was wear the coat inside out.

During this time, Walter and I could no longer live in the apartment we shared with the old couple. They were both ill and needed to use the bathroom all the time. We went to the German police and asked for permission to move to another apartment. They agreed, and we found a one-room apartment on Paulsborner Strasse 7, a home where a Jewish family had once lived and had been deported.

I was lucky with my forced labor assignment, working for a company that made aspirin for the German army. My boss was a good man, willing to risk his own safety for his workers. I worked about ten hours a day. I had to wake up at 5:30 every morning, take a 45-minute trolley ride across town, and then walk another fifteen minutes up a steep hill. But the long hours of work, the long commute, the curfews at night, and the few short hours a day we were

65

allowed to shop left very little time for me to buy groceries, clean the apartment, and prepare meals.

Walter's forced labor assignments changed from day to day. As a strong young man, he was given the hardest jobs. Sometimes he delivered coal, other times he operated a crane at a construction site. Since he went to a different place every day, I never knew where I could find him in an emergency. When Walter and I left our apartment each morning, we could never assume we would see each other again at night. Indeed, after a long day's work, when we did see each other again, we were happy that we were still together.

And then, in the fall of 1941, things took another turn for the worse. In addition to Jews beginning to disappear, never to be seen or heard from again, all the news from the battlefront indicated that the German army was scoring victory after victory.

It was late October, during the Jewish holiday of *Sukkos,* a holiday that we once celebrated with great joy, when Uncle Isidor, my father's unmarried younger brother, went to the synagogue and told us that after services he would join us for a family dinner. It could not be much of a feast because with two years into the war, it was very difficult for us to purchase any special holiday food. Our holiday meal consisted pretty much of potatoes and bread, and maybe noodles. But most important, on this holiday, at least we would be together.

We waited for him. The time came and passed when Uncle Isidor should have shown up. The food grew cold and with each passing moment we all began to fear what was too terrible to say aloud. Finally, we walked in the direction of the synagogue and found a great commotion. We stopped some people and asked what was going on.

"Don't you know?" they said. "The first transport left."

We never saw Uncle Isidor again.

One day we called Walter's parents and grandparents, who all lived together in Mannheim. There was no answer. We kept calling that night and all of the next day, and when no one ever picked up, we became frantic. I took a train to Mannheim to find out what was going on. When I arrived, I found their door sealed, taped, and marked with swastikas.

This sight was appalling. It was especially devastating to find Walter's family gone without a word, without a trace. We knew about concentration camps, and we just knew that people vanished. First, you heard about it happening to an acquaintance, a friend of a friend, someone you had met once years ago. Then closer and closer it came, until it was your uncle, your in-laws, your parents, your sister, your dearest friend. And, worst of all, you didn't know when it would be your turn.

I went to the Mannheim police to ask about Walter's parents and grandparents. They told me only that the Abraham and Strauss families had probably been deported to a camp. I returned to Berlin. In desperation, I went to the American consulate, where I begged for a meeting with the consul. The man who answered the door laughed and told me, "The consul has gone hunting with Goebbels." I felt as if he had spit in my face. No one seemed to care what happened to a few old Jews.

A few weeks later, we found out from the Red Cross that along with 2,000 Jewish residents from Mannheim, Walter's parents and grandparents had been taken to Gurs, an internment camp in France. But there was nothing we could do, no way to communicate with them and no way to save them.

As the war continued, the life that we once had enjoyed in Berlin disappeared. There was no more Kulturbund, no more synagogues, no more movies or concerts for us. It was no longer safe to take long walks as Walter and I had taken on the day we first met. Everything was gray and dismal, so relentlessly grim. Many Jews committed suicide, and some even killed their own children to prevent them from falling into the hands of the Nazis.

Early on in the war, Jews were prohibited from listening to radios, and in July 1941 were forbidden to own telephones. It was extremely dangerous if a Jew was caught doing so, as the penalty could be deportation. But occasionally somebody would take the risk, and we would hear news about the war. Even without phones, talk would spread whenever the Allies had won an important battle. We would hear that France was strong, or that some German planes had just been shot down. That news was like a stimulant giving us the courage to go on.

In the meantime, at my sister Ella's home there were many heated discussions, arguments that centered around Ella's children, Helga, now aged fourteen, and Johnny, aged twelve. We tried to convince her husband, Martin, to reconsider and send their children on the Kinder-transport to join their cousins in England, where they could be safe. Thousands of Jewish children had already been sent from Germany to the United States and other European countries by their parents. My husband and I wasted our breath with Martin. He never wanted to believe how dangerous a time this was and how real the threat of losing our lives was to all of us.

Martin felt very confident and secure because he had fought for Germany during World War I and was even awarded a medal. But more important, he believed the Germans needed workers like him. He did forced labor for the Siemens Company, which produced electronic equipment for the German army. He thought that he was indispensable to the Nazis. It was a fatal error. That whole family died.

I still cannot forgive Martin for his decision, even now, fifty years later. Even when food and other vital supplies were scarce because of the war, Helga would find a way to make a present for her mother's birthday, a beautiful pair of slippers, while Johnny, a genius at anything electric, would fix everything around the house. Helga and Johnny were wonderful, precious children who brought joy to us all. They were so dear to me.

Our daily expectations from life were next to nothing; the tiniest treat made us happy out of all proportion. I can still taste the frankfurter on a string that a friend from Hungary sent me. And one time, I remember that a total stranger gave me a tomato. That was the rarest of things – a fresh tomato in Berlin in the middle of the war. Nobody could have such a thing except maybe Hitler, the vegetarian, but certainly not someone who had been living on rations since 1939. I could not bring myself to eat it right away, but instead felt that it was important to save it for something really special.

And yet, if I were caught with the tomato, that might in itself be enough of an offense to have me sent to the camps for taking a tomato away from a proper German family. I, therefore, tied a long string around this tomato and put it near a window in the back of my apartment. That way, if the doorbell was to ring unexpectedly, I could lower the tomato out the window and not be caught. Then after the danger passed, I could pull the tomato back up again.

I saved the tomato for as long as possible. It nearly spoiled, but eventually Walter and I ate it.

Chapter 9

A Painful Farewell

Jews who had important jobs before the war still couldn't imagine or believe that they would one day disappear and be killed. They wanted to believe that the Nazis still needed them, and that they would always have work, even at places like Auschwitz. I knew better because no one who had been sent there ever returned.

We prayed every night that the Allies would bring a Nazi defeat that would save us. And so every day, with mixed feelings, we waited for the attacks and the bombs to fall. We were afraid of being killed, and we prayed to be saved.

I can't tell you why I wanted a baby so badly. Walter thought I was crazy. He thought that this idea would finally finish us all. He wouldn't hear of it. Jewish lives were being savagely destroyed, Jews were vanishing, and we were totally powerless to escape the horror. Yet, I felt compelled to create a Jewish life, even with the horror around me. My desire and need for a child kept me going; it gave me something to live for.

"How would we manage with a baby?" Walter wanted to know. "Did you think this through? What if we don't survive?" He asked questions that I had no answers for. But I never was the kind of woman to let others talk me out of what I wanted to do.

Walter finally relented. He could no longer withstand my pleas. In the spring of 1942, I became pregnant. Before the deportations began, Walter and I had made a pact. We decided that we would never allow ourselves to be taken on one of those trains. When the dreaded notice came, we would hide. We would go underground. We would become like submarines, German U-boats. Going underground would take a lot of money; we would have to buy everything we needed on the black market. So bit by bit, we set aside any money that we could. We would also need contacts, so we collected names of Germans who might someday be helpful to us. We looked for those who might break the rules, and who had contacts on the black market.

A few years earlier, when it became illegal to use the services of a Jewish accountant, we had found a Dutch accountant who gave us his card with the address of the Dutch embassy written on the back. Our dear friend Willi Melis, also a German, had offered to help us should we ever need him. Willi Melis was a very close friend of the Meyerhoffs, my sister and brother-in-law. He was a Gentile married to a Jew. A well-known architect in Berlin who was against Hitler, he offered refuge to my daughter and me when we had no place to spend the night. Since his Jewish wife was already living under his protection, this made his situation all the more precarious. Through his position as an architect, he was able to secure official letterheads and seals that he used for Walter, which enabled him to travel from place to place for a time. Since Walter's clothes were all in tatters, Willi literally gave my husband the suit off his back. We knew a Jewish doctor who was married to a German woman, and a Jewish woman whose non-Jewish husband worked for the American movie company MGM. A Jew who was married to a Gentile might someday be able to help.

At the time I became pregnant, I was still doing forced labor; therefore, I had official papers that allowed me to ride the trolley.

But I was not permitted to sit, so I would have to stand for the entire trip. Sometimes, as I stood in the trolley wearing my yellow star on my coat, somebody would feel sorry for me and slip an apple or a piece of bread into my bag.

A little luck helps. I worked in a factory that was owned by Herr Starke, who let me hide some important papers and money under one of the floorboards there in case the Nazis came unexpectedly, and I needed to run. He also promised his workers that if he ever knew in advance that the Nazis were coming to take us away, he would warn us first so we could try to escape.

Walter and I planned for the birth of our baby. As a forced laborer, I had a few privileges, such as five grams of coffee and a choice of either getting a midwife or going to the Jewish Hospital in Berlin for the delivery. Walter and I had already decided that when the time came, we would use a midwife and deliver the baby at home instead of going to the Jewish Hospital. We had heard rumors of the terrible things Nazis did to Jewish babies born there. While making these plans, we tried not to think of the Allied bombings, air raids, and shelters that had become a part of our daily lives.

Early in my pregnancy, I began to spot. Dr. Emil Cohen, who was 84 years old, thought the bleeding was very serious. If I wanted to keep the baby, he said I would have to stay in bed for at least six weeks. I did. Here I was doing forced labor, the only thing that kept me out of the concentration camps, and if my boss had reported me sick, I would be on the list for the next train for the camps. But I stayed in bed, determined to have this child.

Herr Starke was a remarkable, decent human being. He let me stay home, held my position for me, and didn't report me to the Nazis. I was also fortunate to have my parents close by. My mother, now 62, was working at a munitions factory; but my father, at the age of 70, was too old and frail to work. So while I lay in bed, my father took care of me. He prepared meals for me and brought them to my bed. My parents were very happy that I was going to have a baby. A new grandchild was something wonderful to look forward to.

Then, in July 1942, they got a letter ordering them to be ready for a transport two weeks later. We knew that the transport would take them to their deaths. My mother understood. She had no illusions.

Even though Walter and I had already made our decision to hide from the Germans, my parents were too old to undertake this. My mother was almost blind; my father was very frail. She, knowing where they would be heading, had accepted their fate. "I'd rather have an ending with terror than terror without an end," she said.

But, of course, we carried on as though a miracle might happen. For those two weeks, I visited my parents every day. I removed the heavy drapes from their apartment, and with the material I sewed two satchels with wide handles, which my mother could open easily. Inside these we hid some jewelry and money, hoping that the Nazis wouldn't find them. Having something valuable might help.

I had planned to give my father a watch. It was a stainless steel watch – very hard to find in those days – that I had bought a few months before. I'd bought the watch on impulse, but after my parents got the letter I knew I would give the watch to my father as my parting gift to him.

The dreaded day came too fast. July 22, 1942, a Tuesday. I couldn't sleep all night. I don't remember what I did about work, whether I asked Herr Starke for the day off, but I was surely not going to pack aspirins for the Nazis that day.

Though it might have been harmful for the unborn baby, I couldn't bring myself to swallow any food so I decided to fast. It was truly a day of dread. At first light, I walked over to my parents' apartment to help them pack. Not to make the situation any worse than it was, they were ready earlier than the appointed time. My father said his morning prayers, as he always did, and packed his prayer shawl and phylacteries into the satchel. That day, his prayers took longer than usual.

My parents were too weak to carry much, so they dressed in several layers of clothing, as much as they could tolerate in the July heat.

The wait was torture. Of all their children, I was the only one with them. Edith was in England; Anna was in the United States; Betty was in Palestine; and Ella, afraid for her family, stayed home. My being in Germany seemed to have taken on an especially poignant meaning. I had to be there to comfort and give them strength. If I had not been there, my parents would have had to go to their doom by themselves.

Suddenly, there was a loud banging on the apartment door. We jumped, even though it was expected. This was it. What we had feared most was upon us. Two Stormtroopers – death escorts – entered. One last look around the apartment, a last embrace. "Have faith," I told them. "We will all pray for a miracle."

The SS shouted out their orders. I helped my parents down the stairs with their luggage. In front of the building was the truck, guards with rifles, and police dogs. No one had yet been loaded into the truck. My parents' names were first on that day's list. We walked to the truck carrying the heavy satchels. The neighborhood people gathered in the street to witness this somber event. I couldn't help myself. I followed my parents onto the truck and sat down with them. We embraced, we cried, we prayed. I wanted to hug into them the lifetime of love that they had showered upon me. My presence on the truck infuriated the guards. They warned me that I could be transported together with my parents if I wanted to. I was sorely tempted. I could not bear the thought of leaving them. The moment I jumped off, the truck began to roll. I followed behind it, walking like a mourner behind a coffin. Then, running for one long city block, I raced to keep up, but in vain.

I turned away and walked home. Weak from not having eaten that day, I lay down on my bed. I could not accept that my parents were gone forever. Over and over, I kept thinking the same thoughts: "Should I go to the transport center and say goodbye again, or is it too great a risk?" Suddenly, it came to me that I had forgotten the watch that I had bought for my father!

I knew the transport would end up at Grosse Hamburger Strasse, where the Jewish community building was. This place, once the center of a thriving Jewish community, was now a place of death and desolation. During the day, trucks pulled in and unloaded cargoes of helpless Jews. At night, when the rest of Berlin was asleep, trains gathered this wretched cargo and started off on their final journey to death.

I lived on the other side of the city. I couldn't ride the trolley or bus. If I were stopped, I would be asked for my identification papers, and I was supposed to be at work. Walking would take all afternoon.

I set out, without wearing my yellow star, walking and continually praying for strength. Finally, the heat was too much for me. I had to risk taking the trolley. I boarded and no one asked any questions, no one noticed me.

Finally, I reached the transport center. I kept my head lowered; I felt that the whole world was looking at me and could see and hear my heart pounding against my chest, but I forced myself to try to be still. I studied the building very carefully and noticed a door where I could easily walk in. To me, this was a sign that I was being watched over by God.

The room I entered was a scene from hell. Hundreds of people crowded together, children wailing, women nursing, men praying aloud, others babbling to themselves. In the midst of all this, I saw my parents. They were close to the entrance, almost as if they had been waiting for me. We embraced again. My father was in shock. My mother told me that just that afternoon the Nazis had come to my father asking about his bank account. They made him sign away everything they had to pay for their trip to Thereseinstadt concentration camp near Prague. My mother signaled me with her eyes not to say anything to further upset him. I took out the watch and presented it to my father. He couldn't believe what he saw. He examined it very carefully, holding it up to get a better look, all the time with a smile on his face. That's how I remember him experiencing his biggest fortune, the last happiness of his life.

All the time, I kept looking at the door. My mother noticed my anxiety and, with eye signals, told me that it was time to leave. We embraced and together said the prayer *Shema Yisrael* (Hear O Israel, Lord our God, the Lord is One). Then I left, slipping out the unguarded door.

After the darkness inside that room, I blinked hard against the light of day. I went home using the same route as I had come, by trolley and by foot, too exhausted even to worry about getting caught. Though I had been with my parents for only a half hour, I felt closer to them than I had ever felt in my life.

That night, Walter and I sat silent and full of sorrow. We had only that night to remember, just one night only to sit shivah to mourn for my parents. We had a plan that we had to carry out immediately. If not, we, along with our unborn child, would suffer the same fate as my parents.

The next night, we ignored the curfew and made our way to my parents' apartment. A Nazi swastika seal was already pasted to the door, meaning that the occupants had been taken to their final destination. No one ever touched this seal. It was like a marker on a fresh grave. I carefully peeled it off. Walter opened the door.

The apartment looked as we had left it the day before, but now it was empty and silent. I thought I would be sick. The furniture and good dishes reminded me of the wonderful holiday and Shabbos meals we had had together. But this was no time to be sick. Our plan was to take what we could carry of my parents' furniture and sell it. We had to concentrate only on surviving and on the baby. This would certainly take money, and selling the furniture would help. The furniture wasn't luxurious, but it was still stylish. Many people in Berlin had been bombed out, and replacing furniture was very difficult, so we were sure to have customers.

We took only the smaller, nicer pieces that could bring in substantial cash. The following night, we snuck back again, and then again. At the end of each night, we'd put back the Nazi seal; and the next night, we carefully peeled it off again. There were several friends that Walter had from his furniture business and they, at great risk, helped us each night. One of the friends used a truck to deliver the furniture to people who would sell it on the black market. I, too, managed to carry some light furniture, using a small hand-cart to pull my load. With our hearts pounding, and terrified every moment that someone might look out from a window and report us to the Nazis, we rolled my parents' furniture through the streets of Berlin. This might be called a miracle. We sold the furniture without being caught.

I don't remember how many Reichsmark we got for the furniture, but the following year, when we started hiding, we had the money we needed for bribes and for living off the black market. The money, along with the last letter my mother wrote to me in which she wished me a happy birthday, was hidden in a special pouch under all my clothing. This money from the furniture was my parents' last gift to me. Even though they never knew it, they helped keep us alive.

Chapter 10

Maria Makes a Vow

When Willi and I settled down to married life, I soon became pregnant and had to stop working at the *Neue Jugend* newspaper. My son Gerhard was born in July 1935. After he was born, I wanted to return to work and found a job with Moserhause, a women's clothing company. My mother-in-law took care of Gerhard up until the time she died, when Gerhard was two years old. I wanted to keep on working, so I found a kindergarten at a convent nearby for my son, and was able to work for a few more years.

A few years later, there was Kristalnacht. I had heard about it, but I just couldn't understand how something so terrible could happen. I immediately thought about my Jewish co-workers at Israel Schmidt und Söhne. I thought about them very often, always wondering what was happening to them during these hard times.

In September 1939, the war started. Germany invaded Poland and other countries in Europe. I was left alone with Gerhard, as Willi was drafted into the army and sent to Poland, where he was a driver for a forest inspector. He was miserable there; he said he was always freezing. After some time, he managed to be transferred back to Berlin.

Because of the war, food was scarce and rationed. I could buy only groceries with my ration coupons. I hated this war, with the separation from Willi, the rationing, and the bombs.

I couldn't stand the Nazi party and what it was doing to my family. Even my Gerhard, at only seven years old, became part of the *Hitlerjugend*, Hitler's movement for all boys. I couldn't stand the thought of him learning to hate Jews or any other people. I went to his youth leader and convinced him to release Gerhard. "He is a very nervous child, always depressed and moody, too sick to be of any use to you," I said. I found out later how dangerous it was for me to take Gerhard out. He could have been taken from me and put into an orphanage, or given to a more "German" family. I could even have been put into prison.

One time, I became really angry because the wife of a Nazi official, who always came to us to collect money for the war, stopped Gerhard as he was going down the stairs in our apartment house. He had greeted her, as I had taught him to, with the words *"Guten Tag"* (have a nice day) instead of the official greeting of *"Heil* Hitler." This woman scolded him saying, "You probably haven't been taught the proper German way to say hello." Poor Gerhard ran home to me crying and very upset. He told me what had happened. Being against Hitler and his Nazis, I made sure that he and Joachim, my second son, would never greet anyone with the words "Heil Hitler." I reassured him that he did the right thing and that he should continue using the traditional German greeting, and that he must not be afraid.

Looking back, I think that was the first time I actually went against Hitler, his Nazis, and his laws.

It was a terrible way of life for us. Everyone was afraid. One person would betray another. I didn't know whom I could trust and who not. Willi always listened to the forbidden radio station. Once, he accidentally left the window open. A policeman who lived very close to us said, "You, Nickel, you are on the black list. Turn off the radio." We were lucky; he did not go to the authorities. From that time on, Willi always kept the window closed, as I had begged him to do.

I, as well, liked to listen to the forbidden radio station where I knew we would hear only the truth about what was going on during the war, and also what was happening to the Jews. Some Germans believed what they heard, while others said it was only propaganda.

Of course, Willi heard about the battles – Germany against England, Germany against France. He always asked how Germany could possibly survive with every country against it. He said that we would never win the war. In the end, he was right. I, too, wondered how long this war could last. I prayed so often that the war would end.

I once saw Hitler drive by, surrounded by guards. I prayed and said, "Dear God, let a bomb fall on the car so that the war will end."

I knew it was not propaganda. I had already seen Jews wearing the yellow Jewish stars. I knew that they were forbidden to sit while riding the bus or streetcars. I saw the words "Forbidden to Jews" written on public benches.

And there were more laws: Gentiles, or "Aryans," couldn't work for Jews. Jewish shops were boycotted. Soon Jews were forced to close their stores. My mother had once bought Gerhard a pair of pants from a clothing store owned by two elderly Jewish ladies. This store, too, had had to close.

Fear of the Nazis grew. One time, when I was in the marketplace, there were long lines of people standing and waiting to buy groceries. Someone waiting in line said the war was gruesome. A Nazi overheard him and immediately pulled him out of the line. Everyone there was afraid to talk. After that, no one spoke up. The Nazis were confident and strong.

I couldn't protest against the Nazis, but I was able to do other things. One day, I was shopping for food at Moritzplatz, where I had heard there would be a special distribution of grapes. Fresh fruit was so difficult to find, and grapes would be a wonderful treat for my family. I bought some, but then I saw some children wearing yellow Jewish stars looking longingly at the grapes in the store window. I knew that grapes and all fresh fruit were forbidden to them. The sight of this upset me very much and made me angry. I looked around to make sure no one was watching me, and as the children passed I quickly gave them my grapes.

Seeing these Jewish children reminded me once again of my former Jewish co-workers with whom I regretted losing contact. I hesitated to search for them, as I knew they were forbidden to be in touch with me, a Gentile.

That is the way it was. I felt so sorry, so helpless, and so angry at that time that I made a vow to myself: I would try to help one Jewish person survive.

Chapter 11

Flowers and Family Feuds

Now, the days were getting shorter, the weather colder, and my belly bigger. Each day that I walked through the streets on my way to and from work, I worried about our plans to hide, when we would stop our forced labor, when we would remove our yellow stars and live as fugitives from the Nazis. I wondered about caring for the baby, about getting clothes and diapers, and how we would be able to manage all of this.

When Walter and I were not at work, we spent time with Ella, Martin, Helga and Johnny who, except for Aunt Marta and Uncle Sally, were the only family we had left in Berlin. Our visits were far from pleasant. Martin was still convinced that his forced labor contributed to the war effort and that it would be their salvation. Aside from that, he believed up to the end that he would continue to work for the Siemens Company, even in Auschwitz. He called me "the lunatic" because of our plans to hide, and my pregnancy. Martin vehemently objected to our plans. He told us, when we again begged him to let us take his children into hiding with us, as they had missed the earlier Kindertransports, that he would never permit Helga and Johnny to join us. I remember him insisting, "Where I go, they will go. A family must stay together." They did.

During these battles, Ella said very little. She would agree to whatever her husband wanted. I was certain he was wrong. Even though I was afraid, I was convinced that hiding offered the only chance for survival.

All these arguments added to my concerns about Helga and Johnny. From June 1942, Jewish children were no longer able to attend school. Both Helga and Johnny had taken jobs to help their parents. Helga did laundry at the Jewish Hospital. Johnny got a job delivering flowers. His boss was a kind person who remembered Johnny's mother, Ella, who used to fill her apartment with fresh flowers from his store every day.

The children, so excited about the imminent arrival of a baby cousin, were eager to do anything they could to help me. As part of their daily routine, they scrounged through the trash bins on the streets to find whatever they thought would be useful for the baby, such as clothes and toys.

Chapter 12

A Christmas Angel Named Maria

I would often take my two sons, Gerhard and Joachim, in the baby carriage when I went shopping for food. One day in November 1942, while I was on my way home from shopping, I saw some women leave a factory on Willibald-Alexis-Strasse. I noticed them because they were all wearing the yellow Jewish star. Among them was one woman who stood out from the others. This woman didn't look Jewish. She had very light blond hair, yet she wore the yellow star that all Jewish people were made to wear. It was easy to see that she was pregnant. She looked sick and appeared to be very tired. I felt very sorry for her. I decided to follow her as she walked down the hill, perhaps to catch the trolley. When I first saw her, I thought to myself that this could be an opportunity for me to help a Jewish person.

Since I saw her leaving the factory, I assumed that was where she worked. I then arranged to do my shopping late in the afternoon at the time I thought she would be finishing her work at the factory. I watched for her, and when I saw her, I would follow her. This went on for several days. I had to be very careful, as I didn't want anyone to notice me around a Jewish person.

The pregnant woman always left her work around the same time in the afternoon, so after a few days had passed, I went over to her and quickly signaled her with my eyes to follow me. She looked startled, but she followed me. I told her that I would like to help her and asked what could I do for her. This woman was extremely frightened when I approached and spoke to her. She said, "Go away, you know you are forbidden to speak to me. We are both in danger."

I answered, "Follow me around the corner to Mittenwalder Strasse where no one can see us and we can talk." She followed me. When we got to that street, the Jewish woman then told me that she would soon have to leave her home. All the streets in her area were being evacuated of Jews.

I thought of the Catholic kindergarten at the convent nearby. My children had gone there for a while, so I asked this woman to go there with me. I knew that these Catholics didn't hate Jews. When we got to the convent, I knocked on the door and a nun answered. I told her that the woman with me was Jewish and that she was pregnant. I asked the nun if she would be able to care for the baby once it was born. The nun said she was sorry, but it would be too dangerous for them to help this pregnant woman. The baby would endanger all the nuns who lived in the convent. I didn't expect this kind of answer from a nun. It was hard for me to believe that they would not save a newborn child. I felt terrible about this. Then I knew that I could neither depend on nor trust anyone to help me save this Jewish woman. It would be up to me, and I became more determined than ever to help.

The Jewish woman must have told her husband about meeting me. But I don't think he believed her, as it was very dangerous for Gentiles to have any contact with Jews. As soon as we saw a person wearing a Jewish star approach, we were ordered to go out of our way to avoid them, not even to look at them.

I was happy that at last I had met a Jewish woman whom I would try to help. I was afraid that an opportunity like this might not come again.

It would soon be Christmas, but because of the war, there were food shortages. The holiday would not be a happy one for anyone. I always thought of that pregnant woman, in danger, and having very little food. Since I only knew where she worked, I thought I would buy some food for her. I bought a basketful of food and went to the factory to look for her. I described the Jewish woman to a man who seemed to be in charge there, and asked him if I would be able to see her. The man told me that he knew whom I was asking about and he would go and get her from the factory.

When she came into the room, she didn't see me right away. When she did, she was very surprised. She was astonished at my searching for her at the factory and that I had brought her some food. She immediately offered to pay for the groceries. I didn't want to accept any money from her, but she insisted. I only wanted to know her name and address so I could continue to help her. At that point, she began to trust me and told me her name and where she lived.

Soon after, I decided to visit Ruth to show her that I had not changed my mind and that I still wanted to do what I could for her. I bought a small bunch of flowers, Lilies of the Valley, and went to her apartment on Paulsborner Strasse.

She and her husband did not expect a visit from me. They looked shocked to see me at their door, especially her husband. Ruth asked me to come in and introduced me to Walter. I again offered my help to both of them.

Ruth told me that she and her husband were planning to go into hiding after the birth of their baby, and that they both needed identity papers. I said I would see what I could do. I asked Ruth for a small picture of herself, and I told her that I would try to have identity papers from the post office made up for her with her picture and my name and address.

Scared, with my heart pounding, I went to the post office with Ruth's picture and asked for identity papers for myself. I was concerned because even though we both had light blond hair, we really

86

didn't look alike. The official looked at the picture for a long time and said that I didn't look like the picture in front of him. I told the official that I was pregnant and that's why I didn't look that sharp. I offered to bring another picture, but he said it wasn't necessary and gave me my new identity papers.

Walter had asked me if I could get him a military pass. That, I knew, would be much more difficult to get, but I said I would see what I could do.

I spoke to my husband about giving his military pass to Walter. Willi was terrified. He told me he couldn't do it. He said, "If I am discovered, the Nazis will put me in front of a wall and shoot me. Do you want to be responsible? You will end up alone with the children." I thought that I really could not put him in that kind of danger. Instead, though, Willi offered to give Walter his driver's license.

It took me about a week to get the postal identity for Ruth and to bring Walter my husband's driver's license. The Abrahams were so grateful. Walter wanted to give me jewelry, but I did not accept it. I told him that he should keep the jewelry, as he might need it later on for something else. I would not take any payment or gift for what I had done. For me, it was important that the Abrahams knew that there were some Germans who were not against the Jews.

I made every effort to visit Ruth as often as I could. She was very nervous and worried about the impending birth of the baby and their hiding. I felt that my visiting with her would calm her down. I told her that I would keep the baby with me for as long as necessary. She needed to be assured that I meant what I said, that I would help them and would continue to do so. Once, Ruth even managed to come visit me in my home. My visits to the Abrahams continued until the baby was born.

Chapter 13

An Encounter with Destiny

Something strange began to happen to me in late November 1942 when I was seven months pregnant. Every day, as I was traveling to work, I got off the trolley and walked up a steep hill to get to my job. I had a feeling that I was being followed. For many days, this uneasy feeling came over me, but as often as I would turn around, I could see no one behind me. But one time I turned around and saw a woman, whom I did not know, following close behind me. She looked very close to my age, a plain, simple, robust woman. She wore an old coat and a thick wool hat, with a scarf wrapped around her head to keep out the bitter cold. She had a kind, gentle look on her face. At first glance, I felt that she was very sympathetic to my plight. She looked perfectly harmless, but to a Jew in these times nothing was harmless. Realizing that I was being followed made me shiver with dread. Hoping desperately that she wasn't really shadowing me, I was shocked when she gestured for me to wait and follow her. Frightened beyond belief, I couldn't move. She rushed to come closer to me. "I want to help you. Have hope," she whispered in my ear as she stroked my cheek. "Please let me help."

Help was certainly what I needed, but how could I trust a promise of help coming out of the clear blue sky, and from a total stranger?

"Go away," I said as I rushed up the hill. "Leave me alone, you know that I am not even permitted to talk to you." I turned away quickly and rushed into the factory, breathing a sigh of relief when the door closed soundly behind me.

But the woman did not leave me alone. I felt her behind me many more times, and occasionally I would catch a glimpse of her out of the corner of my eye. One day, she came upon me so quickly that I could not escape.

"Don't be afraid," she said. "Nearby is a convent. Come with me. You will be safe."

I was worn down by now, too tired to run or fight. This woman had been following me like a shadow for days. At this point, it was obvious that she was not going to give up. I had no choice but to see what she would do. We walked around the block to the convent that was very close to Willibald-Alexis-Strasse. She knocked on the heavy wooden door. After a moment, a woman wearing religious clothing – a long black tunic and a black-and-white head covering – opened the door. I had never been so close to a nun in my life. We went in. There I was, obviously Jewish (wearing my yellow star) and pregnant, with an exhausted, frightened look on my face.

But the woman I had followed wanted the nun to understand exactly what my situation was. She pointed to my star and to my big belly and said, "This pregnant Jewish woman needs your help. You must help her. Don't turn her away."

Not knowing me at all and having spoken just a few words together, this unknown woman, this stranger, was asking the Catholic Church to help a Jew. The nun appeared very troubled. "I cannot endanger the other sisters who live here," she said and rushed us out, closing the heavy wooden door behind us. My protector, whose name I didn't even know, looked very embarrassed and ashamed. She apologized for the Church and then told me that no matter what, she would do her utmost to help me. But I still could not understand why this stranger felt the desire and the need to put herself and perhaps her family in danger by helping me.

"What are your plans for the baby?" she asked. I couldn't tell her. I couldn't divulge to her the plans that Walter and I had made about going into hiding.

"We live from day to day," I said. With that, I hurried off to work.

That night I told Walter about the woman who had been following me and who took me to the convent. To him, my story was too incredible to be true. He worried that I was now making up crazy tales. He feared that, in addition to all our other worries, he now had to worry that his wife was hallucinating.

"What are you doing to us?" he asked. "First you wanted a baby, and now this." I didn't know how to answer. There were no words that I could use to convince him that I had not made up this stranger.

Several days later, my supervisor suddenly came over to me and told me to go to his office immediately. Someone was waiting to see me. I felt as if I'd been struck by a bolt of lightning. Only one thing came to my mind – the Nazis had finally come for me. I was being called first because my family name began with the letter "A." As I walked to the office, the terror in my friends' eyes matched my own. We all thought the same thoughts.

Trembling, I entered the office. The supervisor said, "Shhhh. This woman says she's looking for a Jewish woman, with blond hair, expecting a baby, who comes to work in this factory every day. Only one person that I know fits that description, and that is you. Don't worry, I feel that she is a friend, not an enemy."

The office was full of shadows. Out stepped a woman – the same woman who had been following me, who had taken me to the convent a few days before. She crossed the room and handed me a basket piled high with food: flour, margarine, milk powder, potatoes, and rice. "This was the Christmas ration from the German government to its people. Take it," she said. "I can't enjoy Christmas with my family, knowing that you don't have enough to eat and are carrying a baby."

I was stunned. These foods were precious, almost impossible to find – even on the black market. Even the basket itself was valuable.

"I can't take this," I said. I insisted on paying what it would cost on the black market.

The woman refused. I kept insisting. She saw how stubborn I was, so she finally agreed to accept a few Reichsmark, a trifle for all of this. "And now," she said, "we've come so far, you can certainly trust me and give me your address."

I did trust her, so I told her where I lived. I gave her the ultimate power over us. It was not just this amazing gift of the food basket, but the great risk she had taken to come to the factory to see me. It might be called a miracle.

My supervisor, too, was amazed at the courage of this stranger. When I walked back into the factory, there was silence. Everyone was looking at me. They had thought for sure that I would never return and that they would be called next. I had come back, not only alive but with a large basket of food.

"Do you believe in miracles?" I asked, telling them what had happened in the supervisor's office. In agreement, I heard whispers of the word "miracle." This gesture of kindness brought tears to the eyes of us all.

Before I could go home, I took most of the food and hid it under the floorboard where I kept my money. I didn't want to attract any attention to myself on the trolley or walking down the street. It would appear suspicious for a Jew to be carrying so much food.

That night I told Walter my incredible story. Despite the food I had brought home, he still had difficulty believing me. When I told Ella and Martin, my brother-in-law didn't believe me either. I was already known as being the family crazy. Now, both Walter and Martin called me *"Die Wahnsinnige,"* the lunatic.

Several days passed. Walter and I were home alone on a cold, bitter, night when there was a knock on the door. We were not expecting anyone. Walter and I looked at each other in fright. Every apartment house had an overseer, and part of his job was to pay attention to who came and went, and to report anything out of the ordinary to the Nazis. Who had gotten past our overseer, I wondered. And how? We were terrified, even though the knock was not the hard rap of the Gestapo (German secret police). So, mustering all my courage, I opened the door.

There stood the woman who had followed me, who had already done so much for me. She now stood right at our front door, holding a bunch of Lilies of the Valley.

This felt surreal. Berlin was being bombed day and night. The risk she took to make this long trip, to cross the city of Berlin on this cold winter night to bring me flowers, was unimaginable. Only then did Walter believe me.

Her name, she told us, was Maria Nickel, mother of two small children. She lived on Heimstrasse 10, around the corner from Willibald- Alexis-Strasse, a sixth-floor walk-up apartment. She told us that she was a simple person who had once worked for Jewish people who had been very good to her. All around her she saw what the Germans were doing to the Jews. She was unable to close her eyes and ears to what was happening. She had decided to act, to help a Jew survive.

She offered any kind of help we might need. She said that we could leave our baby on her doorstep. She would pretend the baby was a foundling and raise it as her own until we would be able to care for it. Maria had also assured us that she had discussed this with her husband, who was totally supportive.

A great sense of relief came over Walter as he listened to our new friend speak. Even his breathing became calmer. He had been so against having the baby and was so worried about the double burden of becoming a father and hiding from the Nazis, all at the same time. Now there might be a chance of survival after all.

Walter and I looked at each other. An angel had descended upon us. We didn't want to be greedy, and we didn't want to ask for too much, lest Maria have a change of heart and not want to help us at all. So at this meeting we asked for very little. She told us how to contact her. She was friendly with the baker whose shop was across the street from where she lived. Maria was so poor that she couldn't afford a phone, but if we were ever in great danger, she said we could call the bakery and ask for her, but only in an emergency.

Over the next few weeks, we got to know Maria better. We felt more secure with her and eventually confided our plans to her.

We knew a couple named Stindt, who introduced us to a man named Jahn. He was a tall, serious man, unmarried and in his fifties, who claimed to hate the Nazis. The Stindts knew Jahn as someone who might be helpful. Before the war, Jahn had a simple, unimportant job. But with the war, he suddenly found himself in a new position. He delivered eggs from the countryside to Berlin. Eggs were in short supply – almost a delicacy – and people who wanted the eggs would pay whatever he asked. Jahn realized he had access to something even more important than his eggs: the farmers supplying these eggs could also provide a refuge for people like us. Jahn would become a middleman, and this role would be even more lucrative for him.

For a great deal of money, Jahn would set us up with someone in the countryside where we could hide. We would pose as Berliners whose apartment had been bombed out. It was a simple plan but risky because we all would be exposed and vulnerable. We would have to be even more alert and more cautious than we were now. Everyone who helped us could potentially betray us to the Nazis. Then, not only would we be in danger, but so would Jahn and all who knew what was going on.

At first, we were reluctant to tell Maria about Jahn. What would she think of our paying Jahn to help us escape, while she was doing everything she could without accepting any payment at all?

We finally told Maria what we had worked out with Jahn. Though she felt sorry that we had to pay Jahn, she understood that we needed the type of help that he could provide. To accomplish all of this, we had to have false identity papers.

"I will need your pictures to get these papers for you," Maria said, as always matter-of-fact and eager to help. I gave her my picture. A few days later, with a big smile on her face, she came back with the ID. It had my picture and her name, Maria Nickel.

She would only accept one Reichsmark, fifty *Pfenning*, the fee that the post office had charged. Identity papers, if we'd succeeded in getting them on the black market, would have cost us 300 to 400 Reichsmark. Now I had a new identity, but Walter needed identification papers too. He hesitatingly asked if she could do something to get him a military pass.

Maria didn't say no, but I could tell that his request made her nervous. She told us those papers were very difficult to come by. A few days later she returned, without a military pass but with a sparkle in her eye. She pulled a paper out of her purse. Her husband, Willi, had given his driver's license to her for Walter. Of course, the picture on the license looked nothing like Walter. But still, it would have to do. Any form of identification was better than nothing. Maybe we would be lucky, and it would not be inspected too carefully.

We continued to work, and we waited. Our plans were made. After I gave birth, we would go into hiding.

Although there wasn't much opportunity for a social life, we did occasionally socialize with the Stindts. Theirs was a mixed marriage; the wife was Jewish. Walter and Mr. Stindt were friends from Frankenthal. Frau Stindt believed deeply in astrology. She had a book on the subject and she studied it as if it were her Bible. She asked for the exact times and dates of our births, and then she looked in the book to forecast our future. I felt very uncomfortable with this, as I had been taught not to consult fortunetellers or astrologers. However, Frau Stindt assured us that this was just for fun, entertainment

94

to break the misery of the war and Hitler. However, one day, as she consulted our horoscopes, a serious look came over her face. She told us that a terrible danger would cross our paths in June. I closed my ears to such prophecies.

We also had a friend, an avid Communist named Gabriele Maas, who was the daughter of a Jewish philosophy professor and a Gentile mother. As though sensing our plans to hide, she pulled me aside one day and whispered, "If you and the baby ever find yourselves in an emergency, you can stay with me." I was not able to take her up on her offer because I had found out that the Gestapo was looking for her, and that she herself was in deep trouble.

It was late in November 1942, and I was due to give birth some time in January. Those months were among the worst and most difficult times for us. Both the Americans and the British were bombing Berlin day and night.

At night, when the bombs fell, we went downstairs to the cellar where there was a small shelter underneath the house. Jews were not permitted to enter this shelter, so we had to wait just outside in the little hallway that led to it. During the air raids, we pushed ourselves into the shelter; we could see our German neighbors looking upon us with scorn and disgust as if to say, "You have no right to be here. Go back upstairs."

During the blackouts, there was nothing that could help calm our shattered nerves. If we did light a tiny candle, we were even more afraid that we would be accused of helping the enemy locate their targets. We sat in total darkness, shivering from the cold of the winter and from fear. Hearing the deafening sounds of bombs dropping, we prayed that they would not fall on us. There were times when I was too terrified to move, even to go down to the cellar. Sometimes, when we did go down, I took a little footstool along to sit on. Oddly enough, as frightened as I was, I got used to it. Once in a while, I would be startled to suddenly find Walter tapping my shoulder. All clear. The bombs had stopped. I had fallen asleep on the little stool,

95

Chapter 14

A Newborn and a New Way of Life

Walter and I were so involved with staying alive that we had not really prepared much for the baby's arrival. We had to save every penny for hiding, so very little was left for necessities for the newborn. All that we could gather for the baby was what we could find on the streets of Berlin. We found a castaway baby carriage. All the rubber was worn off the wheels so that you couldn't push it without it making a horrible squeaking noise. The hood was broken and patched all over with tape. We were happy to have it, just as we were happy to find an old horse blanket that we could use as a coverlet for the child.

Since I was in my seventh month, I felt that I had to be seen by a physician. We were unable to find the first doctor whom I had gone to early in my pregnancy. So I went to see Dr. Heller, whom we had known for years. He told me that he would try to be with me when the time came.

I knew I would give birth some time in January, but I had very little knowledge of babies and what giving birth would be like. My mother was gone, and even though Ella had given birth to two children, I could not burden or worry her with questions about pregnancy and birth. I had the name of a midwife who would be able to assist me in case Dr. Heller could not be there. All we knew for certain was that when the time came, I would give birth at home where I felt I would be safer than anywhere else.

But all the planning in the world could not have prepared me for giving birth on January 19, 1943. On the morning of January 18th, Ella, who lived right across the street from me, knocked on my door. She rushed in with terrible news. The Nazis were already on our block, rounding up all the Jews for deportation. "Every house will be searched for Jews," Ella said. "You must make the baby come now. You must jump from the dresser."

I didn't understand her. I wondered why would my being in labor or having the baby earlier be any safer for me.

"Are you crazy?" I answered. "Why should I jump, to end up dying in my own blood? What will I gain?"

We argued a while longer, Ella urging me to induce labor so that I would be able to go into hiding right away. I refused, and nothing was settled. Then she said goodbye and left. Unlike all the countless past goodbyes we had had, this one was to be different.

The Nazis were waiting downstairs for Ella. They had asked her superintendent's wife where she was, and when Ella crossed the street to return to her apartment, the super's wife pointed her out. They immediately took Ella back inside her apartment, where she was made to wait for Martin to return from work and the children to return from their jobs. Ella must have torn herself apart with conflicting emotions, wanting to see her family again but desperately praying that they would not return home.

I would never see any of them again.

But at that time, I hadn't seen anything, and knew nothing of what had happened. It wasn't until a few hours later that a German woman Ella had known came to my door and told me that Ella had begged her to let me know that she, her husband, and both children were taken. Ella had also told her to urge me to leave my apartment immediately.

I would not leave alone. I waited for Walter, who was out doing forced labor. The waiting seemed endless. Alone and scared out of my mind that they would come for me at any time, I spent the day praying that the Gestapo would not catch Walter. Finally, to my great relief, around seven that night, Walter walked in the door.

"Keep your coat on," I said.

He looked at me, his face turning white, reflecting my own terror. "Why?" he asked. "What happened?"

I told him about my sister, her coming to see me in the morning, and of her warning of the roundup. And then I told him that Ella had been caught. "We must leave," I said, as I put on my reversible coat, not showing my yellow star.

And that was how our hiding began.

We didn't know where we would go, what we would do. The streets were still burning from the bombs that had been dropped the night before, and it was bitterly cold. We passed Ella's house and saw the trucks standing and waiting for the Nazis and the dogs to bring more Jews to the transports. The Jews sat in the trucks waiting, shivering in the cold night. But we forced ourselves not to search for my sister. If we saw her and caught her eye, we might talk, to say goodbye, to cry. We dared not draw attention to ourselves, to possibly reveal ourselves as Jews and spoil our own chance for escape. We walked briskly so we wouldn't look suspicious. We pretended that we knew where we were going, showing no fear. We had to make everything look as normal as possible.

We headed to my Aunt Marta and Uncle Sally's apartment, which was about fifteen minutes away. Their granddaughter Mara, my cousin Jutta's daughter, was living with them at the time. Jutta and her husband were in Poland, confined to the Warsaw ghetto, and active in the resistance. They had sent Mara back to Berlin to live with her grandmother for safety.

We knocked and Aunt Marta opened the door, showing both surprise and fear at finding us on her doorstep. "What's the matter?" she asked. "Why are you here?"

I told her that Ella and her family had been taken early that morning, that I had waited for Walter to come back from his work, and that we were going into hiding.

Aunt Marta was in a horrible dilemma. On the one hand, Uncle Sally had been forced by the Nazis to assist in routing out and capturing Jews for transport. On the other hand, here we were, his niece and nephew, seeking refuge under his roof. I am sure he knew about Ella and her family, and perhaps our names were on his list as well. Walter and I were in an awful position. If Uncle Sally came home and found us there, who knew what he might have to do. But Aunt Marta, to her credit, did not make us leave at that moment.

While still with Aunt Marta, very late at night, I started to feel the first pangs of labor. I cried out with pain. Aunt Marta was in tears because she felt so powerless. She wanted to help me, but was terrified of what would happen to her and Mara if Sally came home with the Gestapo and found us there. "You are the only ones left in our family," she said. "I wish I could do something for you. But you are probably safer if you go."

With that, Walter and I bundled up and left her apartment. The streets were still smoldering from the bombs that had fallen, but by some miracle there were no bombs this night. The moon was bright, and we had to be very careful not to walk close to the fires in the streets. The streets were bathed in the light of the moon. We felt naked and vulnerable.

On the way home, we passed a telephone booth. I told Walter that I wanted to call the midwife. I dug the phone number out of one of my pockets and made the call. When I told her who I was and what I wanted, this midwife reacted by screaming at me. "How dare you call me in the middle of the night!" she shrieked.

I didn't really know what to answer her except to say, "We are on the street, and my pains are becoming stronger." She then gave me some instructions that I couldn't follow. She told me to call her when my cervix became as big as a five-mark piece.

At first I didn't understand a word she said. Later, I figured out that she meant the opening where the baby would come out, and she wanted me to be open to a certain point before I called her back. But by then, I was too scared. Walter and I rushed home, realizing that we would have to deliver the baby ourselves.

When we reached our street, we saw that the trucks containing the captive Jews were still there. We were petrified. As we walked into our building and unlocked our apartment door, the apartment seemed strange to us. Just a few hours before, we had left it not knowing if we would ever return. It felt so strange and forbidding to even be there, as if it were no longer our home.

I was now in active labor. Walter tried to deliver the baby. But neither one of us knew what we were doing. And all the while I was screaming with pain. This in itself was dangerous – the Nazis were just outside, perhaps getting ready to collect us – and here I was unable to control my screams. Desperate, Walter went into the bathroom, got a hand towel and stuffed it into my mouth, trying to muffle my cries.

It wasn't long before I realized that the two of us would accomplish nothing. I yelled to him to go to Aunt Marta. "Send her back to me. You stay there and take care of Mara."

He left. Suddenly, I felt very alone for what seemed forever. On the way, he stopped to call the doctor. By the time Aunt Marta came, I could see through the windows that it was almost dawn. A few minutes after Aunt Marta came, Dr. Heller rushed in. At the last possible moment, a doctor had come to deliver the child after all.

It was a baby girl, a healthy baby girl.

"Thank God it's a girl," my aunt said. Normally, no one would care as long as the baby was healthy. But she knew that we now planned to make our escape as fast as possible. If we had had a boy, we would have worried about a circumcision seven days later. Now, luckily, we didn't have that concern.

Dr. Heller insisted that I spend at least three days in bed to regain my strength. He also knew of our plans for going into hiding.

He said he knew of a Jewish woman, already in hiding with her 15-year-old daughter, who could help me. He said they would be grateful for a place to stay, even for just a few nights. I needed the help. If it would be all right with us, he would talk to them and give them our address. They could come and stay with us for a few days. I agreed.

After the birth, my aunt went back to her apartment and gave Walter the wonderful news. He returned to our apartment and when he saw our baby, a look of pure joy came over his face. For the first time, he could see the baby as a real person, not the burden he had originally thought it would be. But then he looked down at the bed where I had just delivered and saw the big, bloody clump of the afterbirth.

Suddenly, he began running around and around crazed. I understood what he was thinking of. For centuries, Jews had been accused of killing Christian babies and using their blood for their Passover holiday. He was petrified that if somebody discovered this afterbirth, who knows what we could be accused of? It could be enough of an excuse to shoot us on the spot. Panicking, Walter picked the afterbirth up in a towel, trying to figure out where he could hide it. Suddenly he stopped and ran out of the apartment. A few minutes later, he returned, empty-handed, with a look of relief. The furnace! Walter had gone down to the basement and had thrown it into the fire. Only then did he feel safe.

Despite the constant danger of our remaining at home, I took Dr. Heller's advice and stayed in bed for three days. This would have been impossible except for my having a certificate from the Ministry of Labor ordering me to return to work after I gave birth. I kept this pinned to my nightgown at all times. I was able to convince myself that the forced labor that Walter and I were doing would keep us off the transport for a while. During that time, Walter contacted Jahn, the egg man. He gave us strict instructions in preparation for our going into hiding. He warned us that the baby must not cry. That would be far too dangerous for all of us. Jahn told us to make the baby sleep by letting her suck on a cork dipped in sweet wine.

Meanwhile, the woman and her teenage daughter came to stay with us. And Walter, for the next few days, continued to go to work. The woman helped me with the little things I needed. So that I could remain in bed, she brought me water and food. She helped me take care of the baby, and was so grateful for a place to stay. She and her daughter had been hiding, but in between looking for new places to stay, they were often forced to spend time out in the freezing cold.

On the second day after the baby was born, Walter got a certificate of the child's birth from the doctor. With this he took his working papers and went to the police station and registered her. At first, it seemed unthinkable. Imagine, announcing to the Nazis that another Jew had been born. We were so unsure of ourselves, not knowing what to do. We understood how great the danger was. Yet we believed it might be enormously risky if we didn't register her birth. All sorts of thoughts entered our minds: What if we were caught with a baby and could not prove that it was ours? What if we were then accused of kidnapping a Gentile baby? Most important, however, was that I had wanted a child – to leave a Jewish child behind – if we should not survive. I wanted her to be officially registered as a Jew. I planned to pin her birth certificate on her blanket, knowing full well that the certificate could mean her death too.

We did not even have a name for this child. But the Germans, with all their efficiency and obsession for record-keeping and details, had thought of everything. As strange as it was, no one at the police station seemed surprised that Walter was registering his daughter's birth as a Jew. In fact, they had a list of approved, very Jewish-sounding names available for him to choose from. On their list were names like Sarah and Taube and Reha. The name that Walter liked best was Reha. He came home with a name for the baby and her birth certificate. He was pleased and relieved to discover that I, too, liked the name Reha.

On the third day after Reha's birth, when Walter came home from work, I heard him calling to the woman who was staying with us, but there was no answer. He came into the bedroom and looked utterly pale but relieved to see Reha and me bundled together.

"Where have they gone?" he asked, out of breath.

"Where has who gone?" I asked. I had been asleep and had just woken up.

"The woman, the woman taking care of you. She's not here, and when I came from work, I found the front door wide open."

The woman and her daughter had left. Not only had they disappeared without a word, but they'd taken some of the things we had prepared for our escape. The horse blanket for the baby was gone, as was our stock of food and some clothes. And they'd left the door wide open for anyone to come in.

Luckily, they hadn't found the money. I always kept it in a corset that I wore all the time, even when I slept.

We were shocked and angry, but part of us understood. They were in hiding too. We were all struggling to survive. They had taken what they needed to increase their chances of survival. They did not have a man with them as I had, and maybe they needed a little edge. But we didn't have time to wonder about them. We had to flee now.

Late that night, Jahn came to take us to the train station. We gave him what he had asked for, five hundred Reichsmark. He counted it quickly and stuffed it into his pocket. He made certain that we'd brought the wine to sedate Reha. His main concern was that the baby might cry.

We had already prepared a few bags containing clothing, photographs, and important papers. Everything that we had collected over the years, such as keepsakes and gifts to each other, all had to be thrown away. We didn't want to leave anything for the Nazis to find. We couldn't risk leaving something that would help them track us down. We were left with just the basic essentials, only what we could carry.

It was freezing cold. We bundled the baby up as best we could, put her in the dilapidated carriage, and went out. The walk to the train station, those four blocks, was the most frightening part of our escape. The carriage with its squeaky wheels made loud scraping sounds with each step. We feared two things: that it would wake our neighbors, who would be suspicious at the sight of three adults and a baby carriage walking late at night, and that the sounds would wake up the baby. We were stealing away from a place where we once belonged. This short walk to the train station seemed to take forever.

When the train finally came into the station, it was packed with soldiers. As Jahn was accustomed to making this trip, he cleared the way for us. The soldiers, seeing the baby carriage, made room for me to sit.

After a four-hour trip, we arrived in Beauleu, the station near Scheiblesburg. It was morning, and in the gray light of winter, we were able to see the open countryside. Jahn led us to a small cottage that was really more like a hut with a moss roof. Goats were wandering all around, and there was an outhouse in the back.

Jahn introduced us to the old woman who lived there. We gave her the money we had agreed upon. She seemed quite satisfied and made us feel very welcome. As we looked around, our hopes rose and fell at the same time. How we would manage to live in this hut we did not know, but for the time being we felt quite safe. We were hundreds of miles away from the transport list that may have had our names on it and the Nazis who were searching for more Jews.

Who would ever think to look for us here?

* * * * *

Postscript

Dr. Bruno Heller (1804–1945)

Dr. Heller, a Jewish gynecologist, and his Gentile wife, Irmgard, helped many persecuted Jewish women escape from the Nazis, especially after October 1941, when the deportations to concentration camps began. He urged his Jewish patients to go into hiding and not let themselves be deported. He managed to find refuge for them among many of his Jewish and non-Jewish patients.

Dr. Heller was arrested on February 23, 1943, and sent to Auschwitz and Sachsenhausen concentration camps. No trace of him has been found since 1945. His wife, Irmgrad, died of heart failure in September 1943.

Chapter 15

Maria Outruns the Russians

I continued to visit Ruth whenever I could. She would soon give birth, and I understood what a difficult time this was for her especially, with no family members to be with her. But before we would meet, I warned her to remove the yellow Jewish star she always wore, for it would be far too dangerous for both of us to be seen together with her wearing it. Often I assured her that whenever she had no place to leave the baby, I would keep it with me for as long as possible.

In January, Walter Abraham called to tell me that Ruth had given birth to a baby girl. I immediately went to see Ruth and the baby, and also met Ruth's aunt Marta, who happened to be there when I came.

I knew they would soon leave Berlin to hide in the countryside. Ruth, fearing that we would lose touch with each other, suggested that I contact her friend Gabriele Maas, who would probably know where to reach the Abrahams, and she in turn would tell them where to reach me.

During this time, the bombings continued. The air raids would begin near Tempelhof Airport, which was close to where I lived. The sirens would start and they were so loud that my son Gerhard would throw himself flat down on the street, trembling and screaming with fear. We were close to being shell-shocked, between fear of the falling bombs and the ear-splitting noise. One bomb hit the front of our building, and we were very lucky not to have been hurt. A year later, in 1944, when the bombing of Berlin was getting worse and worse, all mothers with children under the age of twelve were ordered to leave the city.

We were ordered to pack our belongings and we fled overnight. We were sent to Ostpreussen (East Prussia) and ended up in a small town named Sensburg. We were taken in by a farmer's family and stayed with them for about seven months.

One day, we heard a rumor that the Russians had broken through the German lines and were heading in our direction, but we stayed where we were. About a week later, we were ordered to get our things together and meet at the railroad station the next morning. I didn't know what to do with my good dishes and silverware, so I buried them at the farm the night before we left.

My children and I were terrified, especially when no train would stop for us. They were all so crowded with people fleeing from the Russians just like we were. To make matters worse, we had run out of food. We were in a terrible situation. Finally, we managed to get on an open train that carried sacks of wheat. It didn't help our fears when the railroad people told us that the Russians were just a few miles behind us.

It was a horrible train ride. The train had to stop often because people would stand on the tracks in order to get on the train. By this time we were so hungry that we started to eat the ground wheat from the sacks that were on the train. Poor Joachim soon got diarrhea from eating the wheat.

I don't know why, but after a few days the train stopped, and everyone had to get off. All of us, the women and children, were terribly hungry, thirsty, dirty, and sick with fear as to what would happen next. We knew the Russians were not far away.

The Russians came. They were a gang of barbarians. They did whatever they wanted. I saw them kill children with the butts of their rifles. And then I saw them grab the women and drag them to the woods nearby, where they were raped and then shot.

I knew what was waiting for me. On an impulse, I messed up my hair, smeared mud, dirt – whatever I could find – on my face and body, threw myself on top of my children, and pretended to be dead. I stayed that way for a very long time, how long I don't remember. But I do remember hearing the terrible screams and cries of the women and children. That night, when there were no longer any sounds at all, I arose, picked up my children, and carefully, stealthily, left that area.

The next few weeks were terrifying. I was alone with two small children, running from the bombs and the Russians. I had to get back to Willi as fast as I could. Walking, running, taking an occasional train, and even hitchhiking got us close to Berlin

My husband had remained in Berlin. For the past few years, he had been working in a munitions factory. Somehow, Willi knew we were coming; I don't know how he found out when we would be returning, but when we finally did reach Berlin, Willi was there to meet us with tears of happiness, grateful and relieved that we were all safe and together again.

Chapter 16

A Not-So-Secret Hideout

The hiding place for Walter and Reha and me was in a small farming area. Too small to even be called a village, it was the most primitive place I had ever seen. The house had no water and no electricity. At night we fell asleep to the mournful howling of wolves calling to each other.

We arrived at our new home on January 22, 1943. We had a roof over our heads but not much else. We used oil lamps for light and an outdoor well for water. Before going to bed, I would use the out-house, and I could not help but think I would be eaten alive by wolves. When it snowed, it sometimes took me as long as fifteen minutes to get there. There was no such luxury as toilet paper. If we found a little piece of newspaper blowing in the wind to use, we were thrilled. We could not bathe, but only wash ourselves with rags. Sometimes I went for weeks in the same clothes. I do not remember how we kept the baby in clothing when she grew, or how miserable I must have been washing the baby's diapers under such conditions. Perhaps I have blocked out those memories.

Even though the three of us were together, our lives were very somber. Nothing was cheerful: not our moods, or the countryside, or the weather. When it snowed, we were stuck in our one room. There were days on end without change, with nothing to look forward to. If we found anything to read – a page of a newspaper – we were so happy. We prayed for the war to end and were always on guard and careful not to betray the fact that we were Jews. We lived a secret life, sometimes hardly daring to breathe. Our thoughts were on getting through this, the three of us, all that remained of a once large family. We could not foresee any end. Our only source of pleasure was the joy of being alive and having a longed-for baby.

An old peasant woman took us in. She always wore a kerchief on her head and a big shawl around her shoulders to keep herself warm. She hardly ever smiled, except when she saw the baby. She had no husband and no children.

Her farmhouse in Scheiblesburg was isolated. There were no close neighbors. In the five months that we lived there, I never saw one person come to visit Frau Higgnut, the old woman – not a single neighbor or a friend. Jahn, who had purchased her eggs and brought us to this place, never showed his face in the months we hid there.

This woman's only love was her goats and chickens. She showed them great tenderness and spoke to them all the time, treating them as pets. These animals walked freely around the front yard. The woman was right to treat them so well. It was the goats that provided the milk she used to churn into cheese. When the goats had babies, she would slaughter an older one, cook the meat, and use the skin for something new to wear. There was also a little hatchery where the chickens laid their eggs. Most of the eggs were sold, and the rest were hatched into new chicks. In the spring the chicks ran around the yard. They delighted Reha, who smiled and gurgled whenever she saw them.

The money we paid Frau Higgnut every month must have been significant to her. She didn't know who we were; all she knew was that we would pay her to stay there. If she didn't believe our story – that we had fled Berlin because we were bombed out – she never let on. She was so pleased and grateful to have us with her that she went out of her way to supply us with extra fresh food from her farm, much fresher than what we had gotten in Berlin. Usually our meals were very simple: milk, eggs, butter, bread, potatoes.

One day, she came to us with great excitement. She was able to offer us bacon. Any kind of meat was precious during the war; but to a German, bacon was a special delicacy. To her, it was as if she had offered us a king's banquet. But we could not eat it. Hungry as we were for meat, our kosher traditions would not permit it. Walter and I declined and thanked her, pretending we both had a sudden stomach virus that made all food look sickening. The old woman looked at us in disbelief and shook her head. We were more and more afraid that she would figure out our secret.

Other times, over the months we were there, she offered us bacon again. We always came up with excuses as to why we couldn't eat it. We said we felt sick or we were on a special diet, whatever we could come up with on the spot. We were courteous to her and she to us, but we kept our distance.

The baby was our only joy. We watched her like a living movie, taking pleasure when she first smiled, when she turned over, when she grabbed our fingers, while she slept.

As winter began to thaw, Walter and I felt just secure enough to enjoy our hiding place a little bit and to see the beauty in the simple landscape. There were three rooms in the house, but we had the best one. It had a big window, so from our beds we could see the world outside – the fields and the trees and the animals. When the weather started to get warm, we began to venture out, pushing Reha in the carriage through the fields. We discovered that we were not as isolated as we had thought. Not too far away, there were some neighboring farms.

Some Germans, if they found out you were a Jew, would be happy to sell you to the Nazis. They could turn you in for a handsome reward. However, there were other Germans who were kind and offered help. Their help would someday come in handy.

We were in an area so remote that we felt a little safer from the Nazis. We met some of the nearby farmers, most of whom appeared to be a little better off than the woman we lived with. I asked them if they would like to sell us some food. The one I remember most was Herr Schneider, who lived about fifteen minutes away. We couldn't buy eggs from him because the woman we lived with had eggs too, but sometimes he would sell us butter or special bread. We always paid him a little more than what he asked, to make him happy. We always paid extra to anyone who helped us.

On one of these walks, Walter discovered a rusty old bicycle and bought it from a peasant farmer. We kept the bike parked behind the house, and Walter occasionally got some exercise and fresh air riding the bike along the dirt paths.

No matter how comfortable we felt, there was never a noise that would not set me on edge. Walter was able to relax a little. It was in his nature to be quiet and calm. Not me. If one of the goats sneezed, my heart would pound.

One morning, in June 1943, I woke suddenly to a loud noise and an instant feeling of danger. Reha and Walter were fast asleep. I looked out the window, and there was my worst nightmare – motorcycles and two SS men wearing their black shirts. Suddenly, I remembered the prediction that Frau Stindt had made months before, when she had read my horoscope about danger coming our way in the month of June. Our end had come, I was sure. I didn't look Jewish, but my husband and the baby did. I watched the men jump off their motorcycles, quickly dust off their uniforms, and stomp with their heavy boots up to the front door of the house. I had a few seconds because the old woman would answer the door before leading them to us. I shook Walter awake. "Pray for Reha. Our end has come!"

We didn't even have a moment to pray before the SS men would be in the house. One of the men pounded heavily on the door. They didn't wait for an answer but barged in.

Ruth and her sisters, 1932, from left to right: Edith, Betty, Ella, Anna and Ruth

The Lewins, very early 1930s, from left to right: Uncle Sally, Aunt Martha, their daughters, Marion and Jutta, and their son Herbert.

Walter Abraham, early 1930s

Walter's parents, Elsa and Julius Abraham, early 1938

Ruth Abraham, mid-1930s

Maria Nickel, early 1930s

Reha's cousin, Helga Kessler and Helga's cousin, Mara Markowska

Mr. and Mrs. Bodo Goede, 1936, who had befriended and hid Walter

Ruth and Walter, Spring 1939

Ruth in Palestine, May 1938

Ruth and Walter with Julius and Elsa Abraham, 1939

Walter, Ruth, and Reha, January 1943

Ruth, Reha, and Walter, 1944

Ruth's parents, Frieda and Meyer Fromm, early 1940s

Helga Kessler and her brother John, 1941

Reha in her squeaky carriage, 1943

Ruth and Reha, 1944

Maria and Willi Nickel, April 1965

Celebrating Maria's birthday in Berlin, May 2000. From left to right: Al Sokolow, Reha's husband; Efraim Shachar, Reha's daughter Ellana's husband; Eden, Efraim and Ellana's daughter; John Abraham, Ruth's son, with his daughter, Danielle; Maria Nickel Rimkus; Nicole, Efraim and Ellana's daughter; Reha Abraham Sokolow; Ellana; and Ruth.

"Identity papers! Show us your identity papers!" he said.

In the second it took them to size us up, I could see the tiniest flicker of confusion in their eyes, and it was that slightest uncertainty that might save us. They looked at Walter and saw a man who probably looked like a Jew, and if not a Jew, then certainly a deserter from the army. Then they saw me, with my so-called "Aryan" features, and suddenly they weren't sure.

One of the men stood by the door, his rifle drawn and ready, guarding the exit. The other one stepped forward. Walter fumbled for Willi's driver's license, and handed it over. The guard standing by the door then demanded loudly, "What is your name? What is your address?"

In that instant, I felt like all the air had been sucked out of the room. My heart stopped. Suddenly I realized that Walter hadn't memorized the information on his identity papers. Nor, for that matter, had I memorized the papers that Maria had given me. It was a glaring, foolish error – and it was going to cost us our lives. All the time that we had spent in hiding, bored beyond words, we had stupidly neglected to foresee such a moment. We had never taken the time to study our papers and practice our new identities. And then, sweeping over me, came an even greater panic: in our ignorance, we had put Maria and her husband in a horrible position. Having treated us with such kindness and courage, Maria and Willi could be killed for helping us. Walter's mouth dropped open. But before he could manage to say a word, the officer holding the driver's license read it aloud to the man guarding the door.

The SS man at the door, clearly the boss, considered the information. Then he ordered us to stay where we were. They were going to the police station in town to check out the papers.

They left, and Frau Higgnut, who heard everything, looked at us totally confused. We didn't wait. Walter, being a man, who could be thought of as a deserter, was in double jeopardy. I pointed to the bike. There was not even time to embrace. Walter left, and with him

113

left all my hope. Whether he would escape or we would ever see each other again, it was impossible to know.

Quickly, I grabbed the baby and ran out with her in my arms. It was like leaving the scene of a fire. There was no time to pack. Luckily, I had my corset on, which contained everything of importance to us.

I started in the direction of Herr Schneider's home, the peasant I had made friends with on my springtime walks. But just a few feet down the path I realized that six-month-old Reha was too heavy for me to carry that distance. I quickly ran back and put Reha in the old carriage. Under the carriage was room for a few things, and without even thinking, I grabbed what I could and ran out with the baby carriage. I rushed down the country lane to Herr Schneider's house. When I arrived, I was out of breath.

"Please take me to the station. The child is sick!" I begged, breathing hard.

I don't know if he believed me. But Herr Schneider sensed my urgency and didn't stop to ask me any questions. Without a word, he hitched his horse to the wagon, lifted the baby carriage up, and drove us to the station.

We arrived at the Beauleu train station fifteen minutes after the SS had stood in our room demanding our papers. And there, in front of my eyes, was Walter. It was as if he and I had made a date to meet here. When I saw him, I was reborn. Just at that moment, a train pulled in. I later found out that there were only two trains to Berlin that day. We were truly fortunate to have arrived at the time that the first train, the morning one, came in.

Now we had to get ourselves on that train. When it stopped, a door opened and I rushed up the steps with the baby. Walter followed with the carriage. A man in a uniform held up his hand. "It's overcrowded," he said curtly. "You'll have to wait for the next train."

There was no time to wait. There would be no next train – at least not for us.

"Listen," I pleaded. "Look at this child! Can't you see she's sick? We must get to Berlin to see a doctor, or the baby might die."

In times like this, people had to lie and do anything necessary to survive. The Germans loved babies. German women were supposed to bear as many as they could. It was considered an act of patriotism. The man in the uniform shrugged his shoulders and pointed to the back of the train. "There is only the cattle car," he said.

I clapped my hands in mock delight. "Oh, that would be the best present you could ever give us," I said. "My baby loves animals." And so they opened the cattle car and we got in. Indeed, Reha was delighted to be among the animals.

At most, it had been half an hour, maybe forty-five minutes, since the sound of motorcycles had torn me from my sleep. We bade a silent farewell to Scheiblesburg and to the woman who had sheltered us. We wondered what would happen when the SS returned to the house and found us gone.

We had saved ourselves once again, but there was little relief. During the whole train ride back to Berlin, all we could think about was Maria and Willi. The SS still had Walter's identity papers; they had made their calls and must have discovered what was going on. We had left so suddenly that there was no time to warn Maria. All we could think about now, traveling helplessly alongside the animals, was whether our stupidity and negligence had betrayed this innocent woman and her husband.

We arrived at the *Schlesischer Bahnhof* train station, one of the busiest stations in Berlin. It was filled with soldiers and people traveling. We got to the public phones and had to wait at least half an hour before a phone was available. This time, concerns for our lives and Reha's were secondary. All we wanted to do was to warn Maria and her family of the danger we had put them in.

We jammed our coins in the phone and dialed the number of the bakery across the street from her house. They sent for her and she soon came to the phone. Before I could even talk, she said she knew that I was calling her and why. "I know everything," she said. Her words signaled me to say nothing more. She was the one who felt so confident that she even tried to comfort me. I was concerned that perhaps my phone call to Maria would put her into even more jeopardy. Maria got off the phone quickly, promising that when we would meet, she would tell us everything.

Only later did we find out what had happened. Once the SS men took Walter's false ID to the local police station in Scheiblesburg, they made their calls to Berlin. They easily determined that we were not Herr and Frau Willi Nickel as our papers indicated. Maria and her husband were therefore immediately summoned to appear before the Gestapo. Maria must have realized that we had been found out. There could be no other explanation for such a summons.

When I called Maria at the bakery the next day, she told me that their meeting with the Gestapo had gone well and that they were cleared. One cannot imagine the tremendous relief that Walter and I felt when we heard this.

It was obvious that someone had betrayed us, but to this day we do not know who it was. Living in that hut in Scheiblesberg, we were so isolated from the world that it could not have been mere chance that the Nazis came looking for us.

We were now back in Berlin, free, but with no place to go, no place to hide. Since we had put Maria in so much danger, we felt we couldn't burden her with our present troubles. We could not put her at great risk again.

Chapter 17

Maria Outwits the Gestapo

I remember that immediately after Reha was born, the Abrahams went into hiding. I did not hear from them for several months. The bombings were getting worse and worse in Berlin.

One day, the baker came to get me. I had gotten a phone call. It was Ruth. She was frantic. Ruth told me that two Stormtroopers had caught them in Scheiblesburg. They had managed to escape, but their identity papers were in the hands of the Nazis. Ruth asked if anything had happened to us.

I said, "Yes. Willi and I were ordered to appear before the Gestapo, but we were released after our interrogation."

Willi was very worried. He didn't know what to say or do. I told him that when the Nazis questioned him, he should say that he doesn't know what his wife does during the day, as he leaves the house very early every morning, before seven o'clock, to get to work. And if he is asked anything about Jews, I told him to say Jews don't live near us and that he and I do not know any Jews.

Willi and I went to the Gestapo. Before we left the house, I told him he must drink alcohol – a lot of it – so that when he is questioned, the Nazis will think he is drunk and that he could not really know anything.

We sat and waited in the hallway for a while. I sat on the *Sünderbank,* the bench of sinners. I quickly glanced at the man who was sitting next to me. I thought that he might be a Jew. This man spoke to me and asked me what I had done. "Do you have to go in there? Have you been arrested? Have you been interrogated?" I answered that I had been detained, and asked whether he was too. The man told me his story. He was a lawyer, and a worker attacked him. He had tried to avoid the worker, but the worker accused him of attacking him, and that was the reason he was sitting on the bench next to me. I told him that I had helped someone but would not betray anyone. Then I was called in to where the Gestapo was.

I was afraid, but I don't think I showed it. I knew I had to think of something fast to get out of this situation. I knew that I would have to lie my way out.

I entered the room where I saw six men, all Gestapo, sitting around a very big table. One of the men looked familiar to me. All of them sat there and stared at me. I faced them and said to myself, "You bastards! You'll get nothing out of me."

They asked me if I was Frau Nickel. I said, "Yes, I am."

They asked me, "Where is the Jew Abraham?"

I answered, "Jew! Jew! I don't know any Jews. Where we live, there are no Jews."

The Gestapo asked me the same question again, and I answered, "I cannot tell you because I don't know a Jew called Abraham."

The Gestapo then asked, "How is it that the Jew Abraham had your identity papers? Think it over carefully; the Jews have your papers." They asked me, "How did they get them?" On the spot I came up with a story I believed would fool them.

I told the Gestapo that while sitting on a bench in a park, I had met a tall, slim, dark-haired woman (I had to give an entirely different description than that of Ruth). The Gestapo asked me if she was with a man; I told them she was alone.

118

I said that the woman told me she desperately needed a baby carriage, and in order to get one she needed a birth certificate, which she did not have. She asked me to help her. I said that I felt so sorry for her that I gave her my ration book.

The Gestapo believed me. They immediately understood what had happened. They thought that this dark-haired woman had used my ration book to get identity papers for herself.

I was released. I was free to go but was harshly warned not to ever think about helping a Jew or to have any contact with one. They lectured me about my responsibilities as a German woman, and if I caused any more trouble they said that they would take my children away from me and put them in a home where they would get a proper German upbringing.

After the Gestapo finished with me, they called in Willi. I was a little concerned about Willi being alone with the Gestapo. After all, he knew about what I was doing, and perhaps they would scare him into admitting something. I was lucky that Willi kept to the story that we had gone over several times. He told the Gestapo that he knows nothing; he leaves the house very early every morning to go to work and did not know what I did during the day. Fortunately, they did not keep him very long, and he was released quickly.

Chapter 18

Hiding in Plain Sight

Walter and Reha and I spent our first night back in Berlin sleeping in telephone booths because we had nowhere else to go. In addition, the identity papers that Maria and Willi had so generously provided us with had been seized by the Gestapo. We were without the means to even bluff our way out of danger. Our old neighborhood was the most dangerous place for us to be because people there might recognize us and turn us in. I remembered that in January 1943, just six months before, it was the super's wife who had turned my sister Ella over to the Gestapo. For us, it was better that our old neighbors should think we were dead.

We couldn't even consider going to Aunt Marta. We thought that by now, she and her family were surely gone. On impulse we tried to find Jahn, the egg dealer, who had provided us with a safe haven in Scheiblesburg. We also tried to find the Stindts, but we were not able to.

Desperate to protect our baby, I had no choice but to contact Maria. It was one thing for Walter and me to sleep on park benches or in phone booths, but I couldn't do it to Reha. She needed warmth and a safe place to sleep. Maria, as dangerous as it was for her, took Reha whenever it became impossible to keep her with me. She would put her to bed together with Joachim in his crib.

Sleeping outside was so very terrifying. There were many things to fear: muggers, thieves, wild dogs looking for food, the Nazis, as well as some Jews who, to gain one more day of life, would betray other Jews to the Nazis; and above all, the bombs screeching down day and night.

When one has no choice, one can become used to and tolerate the things that can cause the greatest hardship and aggravation. We became accustomed to the shrieking of the falling bombs. We became accustomed to living on the streets. Sometimes we had to separate and fend for ourselves. Walter would live in movie theaters, streetcars, and wherever he could find refuge for one or two nights. Once, he sat in the lobby of a popular Berlin hotel where many Nazi officials would often gather.

In the summer of 1943, so many people were in need of shelter that sometimes all phone booths were occupied, and we had to sleep on benches in a park. Rain would soak us. Pangs of hunger kept going through us, but still we were able to obtain a minimal amount of food. Weather permitting, we would try to blend in and walk around the city. We certainly feared being caught, but staying in one place would have aroused suspicion and we could well have been discovered. Our major occupation was determining where our next night would be spent.

We never spoke about it, but Walter and I both knew that eventually we would have to separate. The Germans might believe that I was bombed out of my apartment with a baby, but why would Walter, a healthy-looking young man, not be fighting in the war?

Walter was able to make contact with some old German friends, Mr. and Mrs. Bodo Goede, a childless couple in their sixties whom we had known for several years. They lived in a small cottage in Zehlendorf, not too far from Berlin. We knew them from the old days of the farmers' market in Wilmersdorf, where they sold potatoes and other vegetables. My Uncle Isidor had introduced us to them in the

1930s, and our family had become good customers. They had once expressed to us their feelings of shame and disgust over the acts of the Nazis and said they would help us in any way they could.

After Walter and I had been betrayed and fled back to Berlin, Walter stayed with the Goedes as often as he could. When they thought that their neighbors were becoming suspicious, the Goedes arranged for Walter to stay with their friends until they felt it was safe for him to return to them. This elderly couple treated Walter like a son and provided a safe haven for him.

Reha and I stayed together with Walter at the Goedes' for a few nights. But this could never be a permanent arrangement. In far-away Scheiblesburg, we didn't have to be invisible. To an extent, we had the freedom to go out and walk around. But here, so close to Berlin, the situation was very different. Walter would have to keep himself hidden all the time; if there was a knock on the door and Walter happened to be sitting in the kitchen, he had to hide himself immediately. We had heard of Jewish families with babies who had to make the terrible choice of suffocating the baby so that it would not cry out when strangers appeared. We would not put ourselves in the kind of position to ever have to make such a choice. Reha and I would have to find our own way. I would continue to use the excuse of having been bombed out as a reason for being homeless, no ID, and living in the open.

It was in my hands alone to find a new shelter for Reha and myself. I would have to seek the help of strangers. This obviously was a very dangerous thing to do. I would never be able to know for sure which stranger would be the one to turn us in. But I really had no choice.

Now was the time to use the names we had started collecting before we went into hiding, names of Germans and others who might be able to help at any given moment. One of the names I had was that of the Dutch ambassador to Germany. "You can tell him everything," we had been told.

I looked at the address and was shocked to discover that the Dutch ambassador's office was right in the middle of our old neighborhood. I had no choice but to go into a neighborhood where I might be recognized. I walked past the streets that were so familiar to me, pushing my little daughter in her squeaky carriage, keeping my head down. I managed to hold back the tears and the memories of my family who not too long ago had lived on these very streets.

I didn't have an appointment, but when I showed our former accountant's card to the ambassador's secretary, she asked me to take a seat and to wait. After a while, the ambassador beckoned me into his office. I handed him the business card and began to explain why I had come. The ambassador turned the card over, saw his name on it, and sadly shook his head. Then he handed it back.

"What can I do?" he asked.

Reha was sitting on my lap. Looking at the ambassador, in his elegant suit, I was suddenly aware of how the two of us must have looked, even smelled. Reha looked like a little street urchin, smudged with dirt and dressed in rags. My shoes were worn, and my clothes were tattered and covered with stains. We hadn't bathed since we'd left Scheiblesburg; we hadn't had a decent bath since we left Berlin. I had hardly noticed this until now, surrounded by the elegance of the ambassador's office.

Very calmly, I started to explain. "We had a hiding place in the country, but we were betrayed. My entire family has disappeared. We now have nowhere to go."

I had hoped to stay calm, but all my fear and hopelessness suddenly poured out. "Help me! Help me!" I cried. "I'm living on the streets with this baby. You must help me, or I will commit suicide. I will jump out of your window."

The Dutch ambassador was a good man. He offered me his own apartment that was nearby, but I had to decline. It would not be safe for us to stay where we had once lived. He took pity on us and handed me some ration cards for food. "I'm very sorry," he said. "I don't know what else I can do for you."

I took the ration cards and turned to leave, feeling once again alone, desolate, and desperate. Reha, even though she was just six months old, could sense my moods and began to wail. Just then, I heard a woman's voice say, "Wait." It was the ambassador's secretary, Mrs. Schott, who had been listening to my story from behind the door.

"You can stay with me," she said.

Hearing these words was like receiving manna from heaven. Mrs. Schott lived on Nollendorfplatz, on the west side of Berlin, far from my old neighborhood. She told me to wait until she finished work, and then she took me there herself. When I got there, I was so grateful to be off the streets that I almost cried. Mrs. Schott hadn't asked me for money, but I offered it anyway. I wanted to show her that I appreciated the risk she took in bringing me to her home.

She lived on the sixth floor, the top level of her building. Because we were Jews, we could not go down to the shelters when an air raid sounded; we had to stay in her apartment no matter what. During an air raid, I felt the whole building shake and the noise itself was enough to make a person go out of his mind. For me, it was bad enough, but for the baby it was impossible. She started to scream as soon as the first bomb came whistling down out of the sky, and she wouldn't stop. I didn't know what was worse – the noise from the bombs or the screams from the baby which could betray us.

Reha became sick. I looked at her and saw that her face had swollen up. "What is this?" I thought, panicking. "How long has she been like this? Have I been too selfish and absorbed in my own concerns to notice?"

Every parent must have such moments, but for me it was too much to bear. I had to find a doctor I could trust. Fortunately, I had the name of such a physician. I managed to get to him, but when he examined Reha, he said he couldn't help her. He urged me to go to the Charité Hospital with her.

I was terrified. It was one thing to go to a doctor who was known to be trustworthy and who had been recommended, but it was another thing to walk into a big hospital and ask for an appointment. Certainly, I would be asked for identification. To go to such an official place was too great a risk for me to take. But I looked at Reha and realized that it was she who was pulling me through. It was her sweetness that gave me the will to live. If I lost her, I would lose everything.

I didn't want to call Maria again, but I couldn't think of anyone else. As usual, her soft, gentle words calmed me down. "Don't worry," she said, soothing me. "It's easy. I will take Reha to the doctor." She told me to meet her at the Charité. We set a time to meet, just a few hours after I first called her.

When I approached the hospital and saw Maria, a wave of relief came over me. We embraced. It was the first time we had seen each other after my escape from Scheiblesburg, and I had yet to hear how she had managed with the Gestapo. Maria, as my mother would have done, soothed and comforted me. She took Reha into her arms. She looked with concern at Reha's swollen face and began gently to comfort her, too, smoothing her hair and patting her back.

With Reha in her arms, Maria headed up the stairs to the clinic for babies and children. I followed close behind, so relieved that Reha was going to get help, yet desperately wishing that I, her mother, was the one taking care of my own child.

Maria marched up to the desk and announced her name. We sat together, waiting to be called. But when it came time for the doctor to examine Reha, Maria brought her in herself while I sat in the waiting room, my arms empty, my heart pounding.

After a while, Maria, with a smile on her face, came out with Reha. We left as quickly as we could and walked several blocks before Maria handed Reha back to me. "What did the doctor say?"

Maria answered, "Everything will be all right. The doctor said not to worry, she will be all right."

There were no further explanations from Maria, and I wasn't in a position to press for answers after having been helped so graciously. Reha did get better.

But still there remained the pressing problem of where we would go and hide and be able to take refuge from the bombs. I didn't want to complain to Mrs. Schott, but I had to start looking for a new hiding place. As it turned out, she approached me with an idea. She told me about a friend of hers who might be able to help.

Mrs. Schott had a friend named Ruth Martin. Not only did we share the same first name, but we also resembled each other very much. She had been married to an SS officer, but she was now divorced, with a small child, struggling to make ends meet. Perhaps Ruth Martin could help me with a hiding place.

Overnight, arrangements were made by Mrs. Schott, who came back with a message saying that Mrs. Martin had arranged for her aunt to escort me to the countryside, where I would try to find another hiding place. Mrs. Martin would also provide me with new identity papers bearing her name and photograph. The fact that she had been married to an SS officer worried me nonetheless. Therefore, I was not sure that these arrangements would work out. Time, however, was running out for me. In desperation, I handed over the money that Mrs. Martin had asked for.

Walter and I met one more time before Reha and I were to leave Berlin. I was able to call him at the Goedes' where we arranged to meet at the same bench in Preussenpark that we had previously used. There were many things for us to discuss. When I found a new hiding place, I would have to contact Walter and let him know where I was. We set up a secret code that we would use in sending mail to each other. I would use General Delivery at the post office and, with the code, be able to pick up mail, never having to show any identification papers. Walter would try to visit us, if possible, and in the meantime he would keep trading on the black market, raising cash for our hopefully continued survival.

The goodbyes we said this time were much harder and more heart-breaking than any of our previous partings. Once more, we were not sure if we would ever see each other again. Walter picked up little Reha and put her hand to his face and whispered to her, "I love you. Remember Papa, remember Papa." And then, still holding Reha, we embraced as we never had before.

Ruth Martin's aunt escorted us by train to a little town called Neudamm, which was three hours from Berlin. She chattered ceaselessly the entire trip about her niece, about the countryside, about anything and everything. When we reached the end of the line, we got off and she said to me, "Now you are on your own." She got back on the train for the return trip to Berlin.

Unlike Scheiblesburg, Neudamm resembled Löbau, the town in which I was born. I felt totally disoriented. I had no destination in mind. Finally, I asked someone at the station if they could direct me to an area where I might find a room to rent for my little girl and myself. I was told where to look, and I went there.

I walked from house to house, telling people my story, that we were bombed out of our apartment in Berlin, and therefore I was homeless and desperately needed a place to live. Women with young children were being ordered to leave Berlin because of the daily air raids. Everyone knew this, and that made my story believable. Not one house that I went to had the luxury of an extra room that they could rent out. I felt so desperate and discouraged. My feet were killing me, and I almost felt like giving up. It was so difficult, trudging around with the baby carriage, not knowing if I would ever be able to rest. I began to think that Ruth Martin's suggestion of my going into the countryside was not a very good idea, and that I had paid all that money for nothing.

At long last, I came upon a house that was a little bigger than others I passed. It had two floors. The man who answered the door listened to my story. He didn't say yes right away, but he didn't say no either. He wasn't talkative and had an unfriendly look about him, but he was the first person not to turn me down immediately.

"I have a room upstairs," he finally said. "But it is not in very good condition. Sometimes, when it rains, the water will come through. But if you want to rent it, you may."

I took Reha out of the carriage and followed the man up a narrow flight of stairs to the room. Upstairs, I noticed the poisonous Nazi, anti-Semitic newspaper – *Der Stürmer*. This frightened me, but I controlled myself and continued to follow the man to the room. He opened the door and I walked in. He had not exaggerated. The room certainly was in a terrible state of disrepair but, leaky roof or not, it was still a roof over our heads. There was a bed, and I could see the water damage on the ceiling. I wondered just how damp this room would get in winter, but deep inside I was much more concerned about living in a house with a man who read such a newspaper.

The man seemed to notice my hesitation. "Maybe you look more," he said, "and you'll find a better room."

I was afraid that if I hesitated any longer, the offer might disappear. The leak, the *Der Stürmer*, my apprehension – none of these were anything compared to my weariness and the pain in my feet. The baby felt like lead. All I wanted to do was put her down, take off my shoes, and sleep. "No, no. I'm very tired," I said quickly. "The room is fine. How much do you want?" He gave me a price, but I insisted that he take a bit more. He accepted it with a smile of satisfaction on his face. As usual, money had done the trick.

And once again, I had found a place to hide from my pursuers and pray for the war to end fast.

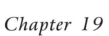

Chapter 19

Cold, Confined, and Confused

The name of the man who had rented the room to me and my daughter was Herr Jonas. He must have been in his sixties, but he acted much older because of an illness which prevented him from working. The finances of the household were dependent upon his wife, who had a job as a minor official distributing ration stamps. The income from the room that we were renting was important to them; that was good, for it assured us a roof over our heads. Because of Jonas' illness, the Germans had assigned them a Polish prisoner of war to help with the household chores.

Frau Jonas, who looked about five years younger than her husband, was a plump, neatly-groomed woman. Her job kept her away all day, but I don't think that her husband missed her. At night, when she came home and I was safely in my room with the door closed, I could hear her complaining to her husband about things that still hadn't been done in the house; this made me even feel a bit sorry for him.

Frau Jonas was addicted to real coffee. Most of what was available during the war was an *Ersatz*, substitute coffee made from chicory which, though it looked like coffee, had none of the taste or aroma that real coffee had. Coffee was indeed a luxury. Whereas normally coffee is measured in pounds, it was now measured in grams. For the true addict like Frau Jonas, chicory never came close.

I learned of her addiction early and made good use of it. Walter was now doing a brisk business dealing in the black market in Berlin. Once I told him of Frau Jonas' coffee addiction, he made trading for coffee his top priority. He sent it to me by mail or sometimes brought it himself when he was able to come see us. When I gave the coffee to her, she would open the package, inhale deeply, and hide it in a secret cupboard. Who knows? The coffee may have been the main reason I was allowed to remain renting my room.

I hadn't noticed him when I first came, but the prisoner who had been assigned to Herr Jonas had an even smaller room, which was next to mine. Herr Jonas was always barking orders at him. "Franz, clean the stables! Franz, feed the animals! Franz, cut the wood!" Although Franz and I were both suspicious of each other at the beginning and kept our distance, we drew closer as the war began to turn against the Nazis. Like me, he had an interest in seeing the Germans lose. He turned out to have the most reliable information about the events of the war.

Though Herr Jonas was ill, that had not prevented him from seeing that a wonderful garden was growing around the house. The back yard was filled with all kinds of fruit-bearing trees. I especially remember the cherry trees that bore delicious sour cherries. Maybe it was because I had so few pleasures during this time, but no cherries I have eaten since have ever come close to the delicious taste of those from the Jonas garden. He also grew vegetables and raised rabbits in a little cage on top of the roof. There were a few cows and horses in a barn out back, and chickens ran freely all over the yard.

Herr Jonas was a patriotic German. Every night he would put on his radio and listen to the latest developments of the war. He grew excited at every German victory and grumbled bitterly about every setback. As much as I could, I avoided all talk of the war. When I had to speak, I tried to be neutral. "War is the most terrible thing. It upsets all normal life," I would say.

My rent didn't include the use of the main kitchen where Frau Jonas did her cooking. I was told to use the cellar kitchen. This was also the place where Franz prepared the food for the animals, and it was freezing cold down there. My meals usually consisted of potatoes and other vegetables. Meat was scarce. Most of the protein I got during those years came from pigeons that I bought from farmers in the area. I would boil them down and feed Reha the pigeon broth, and I would eat the meat, which is kosher.

On occasion, Herr Jonas would kill a rabbit (a non-kosher animal), boil it, and allow us to purchase some of it from him. We were compelled to eat this in order to stay alive.

Despite the danger that we would sometimes put ourselves into, Walter and I tried to meet at least once a month. We needed to be with each other for strength and support in order to survive. Communicating as we did by mail did not give us the connection and resolve that seeing and embracing were able to accomplish. On more than one occasion, I did what might be considered a stupid, foolhardy thing. Together with Reha, I boarded a train to Berlin to see my husband. This was a very scary trip, but the thought that at the end of the train ride I would be with my husband, giving him hope and reassurance of my love, gave me the resolve to do this.

On one of these train trips, Reha was really carrying on and was very cranky and crying for most of the trip. I had no idea how to calm her so that she would stop crying, and I too was in great distress and discomfort at this time. I couldn't bring myself to nurse her in public during the long train ride, so my breasts became so swollen and painful that I had to bite my lips not to scream. The combination of Reha's crankiness and my pain caused me to react in what I thought was normal, which was to slap Reha's rear end. This action triggered outrage in the other women passengers on the train. They verbally assaulted me for having dared to "patch" the baby. They threatened that if I continued to use this method of calming the child, they would do their best to have the baby taken away from me because I was mistreating a German child. Thankfully, the journey was just about over, and when the train stopped, I couldn't wait to get out and away from those women.

My trips to see Walter were as unique as the trips he took on occasion to visit Reha and me at Herr Jonas' farm. Another reason for taking these dangerous trips was that we were both afraid of losing track of each other and being lost forever.

But when I would leave the train station and find my way to the Goedes' and Walter, it was a wonderful reunion, and well worth the risk. It was such a relief to let down my guard and to be together, a whole family. I felt such warmth there, such kindness, the same way I always felt around Maria. Even if you said the wrong thing, they would understand. It was as if we had all grown up together. The only problem was that we couldn't stay for very long. It was too dangerous.

When Walter would come to Neudamm, he was always under Herr Jonas' suspicious eyes. After he would leave, Herr Jonas would look up at me from reading *Der Stürmer* and, in a ridiculing manner, say that neither Walter nor my child resembled me in any way. They look different. He waited to see my reaction, and I would pretend that I did not understand what he was hinting at.

A place I very much feared going to was the doctor's office. There, they demanded real identification. I willed myself not to get sick and if I did become ill, I willed myself to get better. If I felt pain, I tried to ignore it. Pain could mean something serious, but it would be even worse if someone discovered I was a Jew. Better to deal with the laws of nature than the laws of the Nazis.

During the time I lived in Neudamm, I suffered from a terrible pain in my stomach. I thought it might be my gall bladder. Every day after lunch, the pain would attack me. I tried to ignore it as long as I could, but sometimes it would become so intense that I feared that I would die if I didn't see a doctor. I would muster all my courage, put Reha in the carriage, and venture out for help. But sometimes, even though the pain was so severe, I would lose my nerve. I would get part-way to a doctor's office and my fear would make me turn back. I once did get as far as a doctor's examining room, where I was told to undress and wait for the doctor who would then come check my papers and examine me. The very thought of having my papers undergo a doctor's scrutiny made me crazy. I grabbed Reha and ran out of there as quickly as I could.

I finally did find a doctor with whom I felt more at ease and whom I was able to trust. He must have felt a kinship to me because when I blurted out my story from the depths of my excruciating pain, he whispered in my ear that he was not as pure an Aryan as he was thought to be. Then, after a thorough examination, he told me that my pain was not a physical pain but was coming from my nerves, and that I would have to pull myself together and try to calm down. He also recommended that I drink peppermint tea, which would have a calming effect. His advice worked, and the pains subsided.

When Reha was past her first birthday, she began to say a few words. She was able to take a few steps, she giggled and laughed. I was afraid that the lack of toys or other children to play with might make her sad or unruly, but when you don't know any other type of growing up, I guess you can be happy with the things that you do have. Her friends were the large animals on the farm. Her toys were the chickens, the rabbits, and the puppies. With no relatives, grandparents, aunts, uncles, or cousins around, Reha and I were constant companions. She was a very active child, and though she was very easy to take care of, I always had to be on guard lest she fall into some danger.

One day, just for a moment, I went down to the kitchen in the cellar to bring up food. In that brief moment, Reha had crawled out of a window and was hanging precariously from the window-sill. Not wanting to startle her and petrified that she would fall, I tiptoed carefully behind her and was able to bring her back safely into the room.

The more she developed, the more she grew, the more I realized that I had to be extremely careful about every word that came from her lips. Every parent thrills to a child's words, but here there was danger too. One could never tell if she might repeat words that she overheard from me, such as "Jew," or "Nazi," "hiding," or "fear of discovery." Most important, Reha could not know that we were Jewish. There were many things that I would want to do but had to stifle in order that Reha not talk about it. I could not even light a memorial candle for my parents on Yom Kippur (not that I ever knew the day that Yom Kippur occurred). I could not mention our real last name; I could not let her overhear my prayers in Hebrew. She was precocious and could repeat anything that she heard. Judaism existed only as thoughts and memories inside my head, and I couldn't share any of it with my daughter.

Yet she noticed things. One time, I was walking outside when I came across a peasant selling calves' meat. I was thinking of visiting Walter soon in Berlin, and I felt that this would be a much-appreciated gift for the people with whom he was staying. I bought it and spent days in the kitchen in the cellar, cooking and preserving the meat in jars. It was a long process: cooking, heating the jars, making sure the air was out of the jars so that the meat would not spoil and last for quite some time. I was very pleased that I was able to bring the Goedes such a rare treat.

It never occurred to me that what I was doing had caught Reha's attention. Since she was with me constantly and followed me all around, she sensed that my work in the kitchen was far from normal. When we made it to Berlin and presented my gift to the Goedes, Reha popped in and said. "My mother paid a thousand marks for this meat. She worked very hard in the kitchen to cook it." My mouth dropped open. We all laughed. Thankfully, she had not said anything like this anywhere else. How much more careful I became around her.

After a year in my new surroundings, I walked into Neudamm itself from time to time, visited the stores, and even had my hair cut at a beauty parlor. On one of these trips, I witnessed a most disturbing sight.

There was a woman, down on her hands and knees, picking blades of grass out from between the cobblestones. Guarding her were two soldiers with guns pointing straight at her head. How frightening this sight was. The only point of this seemed to be to humiliate her. The townspeople walked by acting as if it was a most normal thing to see. As much as it sickened me to do so, I too acted like the others. But when I walked past her, I felt a tremendous jolt. I recognized her. It was Gabriele Maas, part Jewish, an ardent Communist who had lived near us in Berlin; the same Gabriele who had offered to help me with the baby. For an instant our eyes locked, and Gabriele flashed me a desperate unspoken message: "Don't stop. Keep going." My instinct for survival and all my fears got the best of me, and I walked right past her.

This incident threw me into a deep depression. I couldn't forget the image of Gabriele on her hands and knees, and the guards' guns leveled at her head. This brought home all the more clearly that I could never really feel safe.

The war dragged on. Walter and I were able to see each other less and less frequently. My nerves were shattered and I was consumed with constant fear. My only hope was that the Germans would lose the war. Could I hold out long enough to see an Allied victory?

More and more often I contemplated taking my own life. Only the presence of my baby prevented me from ending it all. One night, very late, I bundled up Reha and started trudging out into the snow-filled forest. The jolting that she felt and the bitter cold that was going through both of us put Reha into a deep sleep, and she did not stir even though I stumbled several times in the snow.

I was deep in the woods, far from any habitation, far from any human life. I screamed and prayed and shouted and yelled and prayed even harder that if we could not be saved, then I wished that an end would come, I don't know how, and wipe us off the face of the earth. I felt relieved at having gotten this madness out of my system but knew that it would envelop me again if things dragged on much longer.

Shaking and still shivering, I turned and headed back. I glanced down and saw that Reha was missing one shoe. I turned back to try to find it, but the swirling snow confused me as to where I had been and was covering up all my old tracks.

I could not forgive myself for having been so careless. I had so succumbed to my depression, that my child's needs went unheeded. How long had her foot been bare?

It was at this point that I prayed not only for my protection but for Reha to be protected from my gross negligence and from my inability to provide for her basic needs. To be forced to buy new shoes, when our supply of money had dwindled so, was a crime for which I could not forgive myself.

I took off one of my gloves and slipped Reha's foot in it. I redoubled my efforts to reach the warmth of our room.

The lost shoe was a sign from heaven. Its message was so clear: Buck up and live!

Chapter 20

Maria Forages for Food

My sons and I were back in Berlin, and at least we were all to-gether. We were being bombed night and day, and it was getting very clear that Germany was going to lose the war.

Willi heard that the Russians were not far away, and he feared that they would soon occupy Berlin. He was afraid that his brand new car, an Opel P4, would be seized by the Russians. He began to take the car apart. He took off the wheels, took out the engine, re-moved the seats, and hid every part of the car in a different place.

About a week later, a Russian officer and two soldiers banged on our door. They had guns that they aimed at Willi. In broken German, the Soviet officers threatened Willi. They told him they would shoot him if his car wasn't ready for them to drive the next morning.

Willi frantically gathered together all the parts of his car and worked all night to put the vehicle back together again. The Russians came to claim the car the next morning and drove it off. Willi never saw his car again. He always believed that someone had denounced us.

But the loss of my husband's car was nothing compared to our lack of food. We were always hungry. There was never enough to eat. I couldn't bear to see my children without food. It had never been so bad. During the past years of the war, we had rationing, food ration coupons, and the black market. But now, close to the end of the war, there was very little food available, and the Germans began to hoard. People left Berlin to go wherever they could find food. These were known as the "hoarding trips."

I had two small children to feed. I had no choice; I, too, went on such trips. I took items that were precious to me, even some clothing. I took whatever I could in exchange for food for my family. Soon, I had nothing left to exchange for food.

The worst trip I had was when I was gone for over twenty hours. I came home late at night with what I thought was ten pounds of grits. I unpacked my bags and, to my horror, found that under a thin layer of grits was sand. I couldn't stop crying.

To have exchanged my valuables for sand was too much to bear.

Chapter 21

A Hard-Won Victory

The war didn't end all at once, nor did we go directly from hiding to freedom. Franz, the Polish prisoner, kept me informed of what was happening. Sometimes the war went well for the Nazis, sometimes it did not. Occasionally, I would hear the news from the Jonas' radio. This was how, in June of 1944, I found out about the Allied invasion of Normandy, the beginning of the end for the Nazis. I was so exuberant, I almost danced with joy. With great difficulty I assumed a serious face and went about as usual.

Recalling my days of deep depression, I was able to understand Jonas' evil moods whenever he heard that the Nazis were being defeated. At those times, it was almost impossible to be anywhere near him. By early 1945, he was a totally broken man. The fear in the voices of the Nazi radio commentators made its way into every German home. The Allies had started moving into German territory. Before long, the day that all of us had been praying for would arrive. Liberation was near, but no one knew what it would bring.

The Nazi propaganda machine kept exhorting the people to be brave, to fight fiercely and not give up. But in the areas close to German-occupied territories, the message was different. We, in Neudamm, so close to the Polish border, were told to pull back towards central Germany.

The propagandists made us fear the Russians. They were barbarians, the Nazis said, who would rape the women and shoot the men on sight. Jonas wanted us to evacuate using the small farm carts used for gathering produce from the fields. "We should start moving," he would say. "You and the child will come with us on the carts. It is beginning to be too dangerous for us to stay here; we have to leave."

I really didn't know what to do. I hadn't heard from Walter. If I left Neudamm with Jonas and his wife, Walter might never find me. If Jonas left without me, I would have to face the Russians alone. I tried to put off leaving with Jonas for as long as I could, hoping my excuses would hold out until I heard from Walter. "I am too weak and tired to go on a long trip," I said. "Who knows whether it will be better where we go?"

Time was running out. The German government had formed the *Volkssturm* – a people's army – a desperate act, drafting every man into the German army, even those who were disabled and handicapped. A man like Walter, looking very able-bodied, would certainly not be safe on the streets of Berlin.

Late one night, I was awakened by a loud crack. I looked up and saw that a rock had shattered my window. Still half asleep, my first thought was of Kristalnacht. Suddenly, from outside, I heard a voice calling, "Ruth! Ruth!"

It was Walter. Never had a wife been so happy to see her husband. Quickly, I ran downstairs and let him in. Amazingly, no one – not even Reha – had woken up from the noise. In the quiet of the night, we whispered, catching up on news, and then cleaned up the shattered pieces of glass. We got under the covers and waited for whatever would happen next. Walter had left Berlin just in time.

The roar of airplanes overhead awakened us in the morning. People used to say that the Russians had the oldest and noisiest airplanes. It was true. When they started dropping bombs, memories of Berlin came flooding back. We all fled the house, running for a small underground bunker that Jonas had prepared a few months before.

For a day and a night, the six of us – Jonas, his wife, Franz, Walter, Reha, and I – took our places on the dirt floor of the bunker and waited. Everyone tried to comfort Reha, who was crying from all the noise. We suddenly realized that it had become very quiet. The bombs had stopped falling. But when we opened the door of the bunker, we heard a different type of noise, the sound of horses running, a stampede of horses pounding the earth. In a panic, we all ran to the first place we saw, which was the stable.

Jonas kept insisting in the face of the approaching Russian cavalry that we all leave. He could not understand my hesitancy. It was then that I told him what I had been afraid to divulge to him all along, that the three of us were Jewish. And that had been our only "crime" against the Nazis. Jonas and his wife didn't seem to be surprised. They said that they had suspected something but decided not to do anything about it.

And so the tables turned. We had kept our dangerous secret for such a long time. It may have been hinted at, but it was never spoken. For the past two years, while we prayed for the Allies to win the war, Jonas had been in control of our lives. With one word, he could have had us deported to our death. He didn't, and now Jonas and his wife, on their hands and knees, kissing our shoes, were begging us to report them as decent Germans.

"Save us! Save us!" Jonas pleaded. "We saved you. From the beginning, I always suspected you. Remember, I said that the child looks so different, that your husband looks so different? We felt that you must be Jews. But we did not betray you. Now, please, save us!"

What does one say to such a strange turn of events? Nothing – only pity and embarrassment. And it had its effect. Jonas was right. He had sheltered us. He hadn't acted on his suspicions. Whatever he thought of the Jews, whatever suspicions he might have had about

Walter and the baby, Jonas had turned his head the other way. He had acted as a human being first, a German second. Now, with the moment of judgment upon us, I made up my mind. I, too, would act as a human being and do what I could to help save Jonas and his wife.

Suddenly, the door to the stable flew open and we found ourselves face to face with Russian soldiers on horseback and rifles pointed at us. Their eyes were wild, they were panting as if with exhilaration. Some were drunk. It didn't feel as though we were being liberated. Here we were, finally, at the end of our hiding – and just a hair trigger away from being shot. One wrong move and we could all be dead.

Walter and I began to shout, "*Jevri! Jevri!* We're Jewish! We're Jewish! Don't shoot!" I pulled out a small prayer book, which I'd always kept carefully hidden, to show the Russians the Hebrew prayers.

Seeing this, the Russians relaxed somewhat. Their guns were still pointed at us, but their faces looked a bit less menacing. Franz, the Polish prisoner, spoke a bit of Russian. He told them he was a Polish prisoner of war. He told them that we were Jews, hiding from Hitler.

"And who are they?" one of the Russian soldiers asked, gesturing with his rifle at the Jonases. Jonas was speechless. I saw the same terror on his face that I had felt these past few years of hiding. Now I sympathized with him, human being to human being. I didn't want to see him killed.

"They are the people who hid us during the war," I said quickly with Franz translating. "They were good to us. They gave us food. They are not Nazis."

By instinct, I stripped off my wristwatch and handed it to one of the Russian soldiers. Walter did the same. We hoped that our watches would do the trick and that they would leave Jonas and his wife alone. It seemed to work. The Russian soldiers relaxed their rifles a bit more. Noticing that, I decided to offer a little extra. "Wait, wait. Give me a moment to go upstairs," I said. I rushed up to my room to find a few more valuables, to give whatever I could to save Jonas and his wife.

The Russian soldiers left, taking our valuables with them. We didn't know what would come next. All over Neudamm, Russian soldiers were barging into houses, interrogating people, and looking for Nazis. It was complete bedlam. The only thing that seemed to matter was who had a gun.

Everyone waited to be told what to do. Then, from loudspeakers mounted on trucks, I heard Russian officers make announcements. Their instructions came in many languages – Russian, Polish, and German. Prisoners of war, like Franz, were freed.

People were ordered to appear in the center of the town with their identity papers, where the Russians had organized a transport to safety for people such as us who were oppressed by the Nazis. I don't recall exactly how, but we were issued some papers stating that we were Jews.

I didn't want to go. I felt completely drained and weak. I had begun to cough a lot and I couldn't shake it. All I wanted to do was to cover my head and sleep, and sleep, and sleep.

Walter convinced me otherwise. We had no ties to Neudamm, and staying behind could have put the idea into the Russians' heads that we really were their enemy. I kept making excuses to Walter as to why we should not go. I was too weak. It was too cold. I was still coughing. It would be too difficult a journey for Reha. Nothing helped. Walter insisted that we had no choice, so we went.

Out of all this chaos, my friend Gabriele Maas suddenly appeared. I wondered what had happened to her. With liberation, Gabriele had been released from prison and she told me that she had searched for me from house to house. Seeing her again gave me the greatest joy and pleasure. We embraced, tears rolling down our cheeks, crying for what we had lost.

"Come with us," we begged Gabriele. "We will all make a new start together." I thought that she, as a single woman, would jump at such an offer, but she turned us down. She said she would take her chances where she was. Walter cautioned her that if she stayed behind, she stood the risk of being misunderstood, or worse, molested. She could not be persuaded.

Walter, Reha, and I went to the center of town, from which we were all going to be transported. To the best of my knowledge, there were no other Jews around, nor were there any other women or children. We had started our hiding with very little, and we had less now – bits of clothing, our papers, and the ever-present squeaky, battered baby carriage.

There were more announcements. We were told that we could enter any German home and take what we wanted – the spoils of war— our turn for revenge, to plunder. The Germans had fled when they knew that the Russians were approaching. They would never come back. We did not have any compunction about going into a German house and seeing if there was anything there that we could use.

We entered a few of the German houses and looked around. There, in some of the pantries, were containers filled with rice, potatoes, oats, and other staples. We took this food that we desperately needed. And then I spotted something that I did truly want: a beautiful little red knitted coat that would keep Reha so very, very warm. I held it up to Reha. It looked like it had been made for her. I slipped her arms in.

Chapter 22

Walking on Thin Ice

We began to travel. We were lucky because Reha, who was just two years old, and I were permitted to go on a farm cart, of which there were several. With few exceptions, these carts were meant mostly for the Russian military officers. Everyone else, including Walter, had to walk.

The road was rough and bumpy, and we shivered in the freezing cold. We were not told where we were going or how long our journey would take. No matter what, we were free and did not have to fear being Jewish.

We traveled in this manner for three or four days with many stops because the wagons kept breaking down. When it became dark and we stopped for the night, we were permitted to sleep in any house we cared to. All the houses were deserted. Not one human being was in sight. It was an odd feeling to enter and use the beds of total strangers. But it was either that or sleep on the floor. Once again, most of the houses had food in them left over when the owners fled from the approaching Russian army. After a while, this way of life seemed normal to us.

We woke up in the mornings a bit frightened, and only relaxed when we saw that the transport and wagons had not left us behind. Reha liked the wagon. She liked looking all over at the change of scenery. "Where are we going today, Mommy?" she would ask, but neither Walter nor I was able to answer.

One day we came to a river that was frozen over. On the other side was the city of Landsberg, close to Küstrin. After much discussion among themselves, the Russians decided that it would be too dangerous to try to cross the river with the wagons. We would all have to get out and cross by foot. Walter helped me make Reha comfortable in the carriage, and he started to go on ahead with the other men. I walked slowly and, pushing the carriage, fell farther and farther behind the main group.

Suddenly, without warning, the front wheels of the carriage seemed to sink into the ice and I felt as if we were surely going to fall in and drown. I shouted and screamed for help. Walter and the group of men he was with were too far ahead to hear me. But some people nearby, hearing me and seeing what was happening, rushed over and were able to pull Reha in the carriage and me from this section of the ice. Walter, suddenly sensing that something was wrong, came rushing back to help me and to walk along with us.

My feet were frozen, and Reha could not be comforted, yet we had to keep going until we reached the other side of the river. With every step, I was overcome with fear that once again the ice would crack.

To my great relief, we reached the other side safely.

This episode on the ice-covered river was so symbolic. Going from safety to danger. Falling part way in, being helped out, always by strangers. This event seemed to be a quick flashback of the life we had been leading.

Chapter 23

Liberated but Not Free

Our transport stopped in Landsberg, where the Russians had set up a military base. Once again, we had to have our papers examined to prove that we were not and never had been Nazis. Once we were cleared, we were permitted to go into the town and choose any house we wanted to and make a home for ourselves.

Not caring what the house looked like but so desperately in need of shelter, Walter and I were ready to take the first empty house we came to. We had no day-to-day plan but knew that our ultimate goal was to reach Berlin. On the way to searching for a place to live, we had come across some Russian soldiers who were slaughtering a cow.

The very thought of having fresh meat bolstered my courage to the point where I went up to those Russian soldiers and told them that I was Jewish and had escaped the Nazis. I then asked for some of the meat they had slaughtered for my little daughter and husband. They told me that I should come back there the next day and they would make some of it available to me. We continued looking for a house to live in and looked forward to getting real food the next day.

We finally located a house where we would be able to rest and recover from our journey. We all fell into a very deep sleep and were

147

awakened early the next morning by a loud knocking at the door. Knocking or banging on a door was a sound that every person being hunted was afraid of. Yet, I felt safe. We were with the Allies and not with the Nazis.

Walter opened the door, and two Russian officers marched in. They searched through all our possessions, even ripping apart the seams of the one good suit jacket that I still had left. They pulled out the shoulder pads and even took those apart. There was nothing there for them to find. They finally left but said they had to take my husband with them.

To keep my spirits up, I convinced myself that this was a normal procedure. That it would take just a couple of hours, and Walter would be safe and would soon be back with us.

To distract myself, I spent the morning setting up house. The clothes that had gotten wet from the icy river had to be hung up and dried. I went through the pantry to see what food was available. At first, using the stove and drawing water were a puzzle to me. But I was able to figure it out. Reha was wandering about the house, cheerfully discovering new things with which to play. A few hours passed and Walter was still not back. Fear began to creep through my very bones. The explanation that I had given myself had fallen apart. By nightfall, there was no denying it. Walter was gone. Reha and I were once again on our own.

Early the next morning, I took Reha and rushed to Russian headquarters. I was hysterical. I was not permitted into the building. I kept demanding information about my husband, and I kept demanding to see the Kommandant. The only response I got was to be quiet and wait. By midday, I knew that my waiting was totally in vain. I took Reha and went back to our house.

After everything we had been through, after having escaped from the Nazis and having come so close to freedom, my husband was taken away. In my distress, my mind went back to the early morning invasion of our house the day before, and how upset I was when the officers had ripped the seams of my jacket. I had lost so much already: parents, relatives, loved ones, so many, many people, and here I was agonizing over a piece of clothing. And suddenly I realized what it was that was bothering me. It wasn't the ripped seams or the searching of the house, it was the idea that we were being looked upon as German spies; the search had been conducted to try to gather evidence against us. I even fantasized that my asking for meat had singled us out and set us up to be accused of being spies.

My main obsession now was finding Walter and getting him out of the clutches of the Russians. I thought back to the time when I had been successful in getting Walter's father released from Dachau, and I felt now that I had to embark on a similar mission for Walter. I would once again try to get to see the Kommandant and, if I was able to, I would try to convince him that we were not spies, that we were oppressed Jews, and that Walter's arrest was a horrible error.

In the morning, I took Reha and made my way to the headquarters building. Using every argument I could think of, I pleaded and I begged for the guards to allow me to approach the Kommandant's office. The only answer that I was given was to wait. And wait I did, not just that day, but many days. Reha and I would arrive early in the morning. At noontime, I would take her back to the house and attend to her needs. After her nap I would once again return to my post in front of the headquarters building, again pleading and begging for an audience with the Kommandant.

With each succeeding day, I was becoming more desperate, more frantic. I knew I was falling apart. In addition to my pleading and begging, I also asked for mercy for my little child, who perhaps was so close to becoming fatherless. Again, with no success at all, I would return home discouraged, despondent and defeated, empty, more hopeless than I had ever felt.

One day, as we were leaving headquarters, I saw a sight that I could hardly believe. A line of prisoners was coming out of the headquarters building, each one carrying a pail that was the toilet they had used during the night. They emptied these into a nearby ditch. The smell was horrific. The men looked like relics of human beings. Their last shred of dignity had been taken away from them.

There among them, was my husband. I was in shock. As the line turned to go back into the building, Walter looked up. I felt sure that he would recognize me. To get his attention I picked up Reha, who was wearing the red coat that we had acquired some time before. Surely, this red coat would stand out like a beacon. He couldn't help but see it. He would recognize her. He would see us, and he would know that we had not deserted him, that we were here waiting, hoping and praying for his release.

"Papa, Papa," I called. Holding Reha up as high as I could, she too called out, "Papa, Papa."

He glanced in our direction, and I knew in my heart that he had seen us. At that moment, one of the guards pushed and shoved him to keep the line going. And the men re-entered the building. Who could have thought that Walter was in this building, so very close to our home?

Seeing Walter made my visits more and more urgent, and I became more brazen and more outspoken and more demanding to the point where I was told that if I did not stop, then something drastic would happen to me. I didn't stop my daily trips, but I was careful and became quiet, less demanding, and less abusive to the soldiers.

More than six weeks had passed since Walter was taken, and it was spring. Meeting defeat every day brought me to the point of total despair. I had no family that I could go to for help and support. Reha and I were totally alone. Waiting and praying for Walter's return was what kept us going. Our daily routine of finding food and maintaining our little home was the type of endurance that kept me rational and sane. My physical and mental strength were leaving me, so much so that one day, while walking, I collapsed in the street.

When I came to and looked up, I saw a Russian soldier standing over me. Speaking in broken German, he offered to help. Except for Reha, he was the first person in so many months with whom I was able to converse.

I told him who I was. I told him about Walter. I told him about the lack of food. I told him of my despair. I poured out my soul to him. I told him everything, even telling him that I feared that it was the KGB that was after us. He stiffened at hearing those initials and told me that if I ever repeated them, he would not help me at all. It seemed that even mentioning this Russian secret police organization was enough to strike fear in the hearts of anyone. He confided to me that he too was Jewish, and that he would do whatever he could to help us. I had survived Hitler, and now there was another menace in the foreground.

"You must see a doctor," the soldier said. "That is the first thing you have to do. Nearby is a German doctor." He led me by the arm to a one-room clinic a few blocks away. The German doctor turned out to be a woman. The soldier demanded that she examine me right away, and he pulled out his gun to show he meant business. "And if she dies, I will shoot you," he told her.

I was examined, and very quickly she discovered the source of my problem. I was pregnant. It was no wonder I had been so weak. When I heard this diagnosis, my sobs came pouring out; it was simply more than I could bear. Not knowing if my husband would ever come back, I explained to her that in no way could I ever go through with this pregnancy. I was totally alone except for my baby, Reha, and I pleaded with the doctor to help me.

Having no choice, the doctor did help me but pointed out that her little clinic was very poorly equipped to handle this procedure. Still, she did it, and when it was over, she insisted that I stay there overnight. This meant that Reha would have to remain there with me.

151

The next day, the Jewish soldier came back and escorted us home. That's when he told me that he had been a political prisoner for ten years in Russia and cautioned me again never to even mention the KGB. He left us at the house and I never saw him again.

For over a week I kept off my feet as much as possible and tried to recover. Reha must have sensed my despair, as she was especially good and was able to occupy herself for many hours at a time while I rested. When I finally went out of the house, I saw much activity among the Russian soldiers. They kept gesturing and speaking in their language that I did not understand. But I kept hearing the words "President Roosevelt" being repeated over and over again. On April 12, 1945, President Roosevelt died, and the presidency was in the hands of Harry Truman.

On April 30, two-and-a-half weeks later, I discovered that Russian troops had broken through into Berlin itself and that Hitler had committed suicide. But all this had happened far away. Reha and I were as isolated as we ever were, and my husband was still among the missing.

Instead of being overjoyed and thrilled at the prospect of finally being free from the Nazis and their atrocities, I fell deeper and deeper into what I realized was depression. It seemed that all hope was gone. There was no sign of Walter. Reha needed more and more of my attention and patience, which I did not have, and there was no human being nearby to whom I could talk and who would tell me, "Ruth, snap out of it!" I was obsessed with the idea that my begging for a piece of meat had started off a series of events that ended with my husband's being gone, and there was no one there to tell me how foolish it was to have these thoughts.

One day, a man whom I recognized as a worker in the area came knocking at my window. He told me that there was a beggar outside my house who wanted a piece of bread. "Tell him to go away," I said. "I have nothing to give him." The workman returned and insisted that the beggar would not leave, and could I please spare even the smallest bit of bread for him.

"No," I cried. "I don't have bread! Even for my child, I don't have bread."

And suddenly I heard a new knock, this time on the door to our house. I tried to ignore it, but the knocking continued. Whoever was knocking was very persistent. I couldn't stand the incessant knocking and banging, so with Reha fearfully clinging to my skirts, I went to the door, opened it, and there stood the beggar himself.

He was filthy. His body reeked with horrible odors. His breathing was more like wheezing and coughing. He looked like he was a very sick man. His clothing was torn, tattered, and in many places did not properly cover his body. His hair, falling all over his face and ears, was almost too filthy to describe. He raised his eyes. Some clothing fell away from his head and neck. I gasped. Was this my husband, Walter? Reha, still holding onto my skirts, looked at the man and started crying and whining. "Make him go! Make him go!" she said.

You can imagine the joy, the happiness I felt that once again Walter and I were together. But the sight of the crawling lice scurrying all over his head and body revolted me. I could hardly bear to look. But this was my husband, and I had to take care of him and help him, no matter the risk.

It was well known that lice were carriers of the deadly disease typhus. I knew what I had to do. His clothing had to be burned. The lice had to be killed, and medical care had to be found. I had seen a bottle of concentrated vinegar in the house when we had first arrived. I took it to the well, pumped up water, and made a mixture of the concentrate and the water. I went back to Walter and helped him get rid of all of his clothing. I poured the vinegar mixture over him and helped wash the lice from his body. He felt very warm. He was certainly running a high fever. When I was sure that the lice were gone, I let him into the house, where he was washed and thoroughly cleaned. I made him as comfortable as I could. Reha had finally calmed down, so I left the house to try to find a doctor.

I had heard of a Russian military hospital not too far away. I ran there and screamed and yelled for help. A few Russian officers came over and wanted to know what was happening. In my broken Russian-German, I explained that I was Jewish, and at my home was my little child and a very sick husband. They wanted to know more about his sickness, so I said they should come with me and they would see for themselves. They did come, and when they saw the condition that Walter was in and the possibility of his having typhus and spreading it, they took the three of us back to the hospital and put us all together in a quarantine room, where we stayed for 30 days. Walter received good medical care, and slowly he began to regain his strength.

When Walter was well enough to talk, he began to tell me a little about his imprisonment. He had seen Reha and the red coat that morning outside of headquarters, and it was the sight of the two of us, still alive, waiting for him, that kept his spirits up during the entire time of his imprisonment. He also was able to tell me why he had been released. He had insisted all along that he was a Jew and not a Nazi spy. Towards the end, the Russians brought in a Jewish physician, who came to Walter's cell with a prayer book. Walter had to prove his ability to read Hebrew. When that test was passed, the doctor examined him to verify that he was circumcised. With these two proofs, the Russians released him, and he was somehow able to find the little house from which he had been taken and where, miraculously, we still lived.

Our quarantine in the hospital and the war itself ended simultaneously. We were very eager to get to Berlin and were able to get a ride there in a truck with Russian soldiers. On the way there, we went through what once was called the city of Küstrin. A major battle must have taken place there just recently, for the fields were strewn with decaying bodies of humans and animals. It was a ghastly, heart-rending sight.

When we finally arrived in Berlin, the soldiers asked us where we wanted to be dropped off. There was only one place we could think of – the old neighborhood. When we got there, we asked the soldiers to drive slowly so that we could take in the old familiar sites and the places that we remembered so well. I could see many of the bombed-out buildings, but I could not see the Jewish stores, the synagogues, and other places that we knew so well. They had all disappeared. This was our old neighborhood, but it was empty of all the people whom we had loved and who had once loved us.

I suddenly shouted for the driver to stop. We had just come to the street where Anna, who had immigrated to Philadelphia, had lived. There was her old apartment building, still standing. Out in front was an old man whom I recognized as the building's superintendent. I left the truck, went over to him, and he recognized me too. I told him that we had been hiding during the war and had just now come back to Berlin, and we were without a place to live

"You know, it's funny," the super said. "Your sister's old apartment is vacant." And so, without another thought, it was settled. We left the truck with our tiny store of possessions and thanked the soldiers for their trouble. The super let us into the apartment and gave us the key. He even helped us scrounge for a few mattresses and chairs.

Now that we were settled with a place to live, we renewed our efforts to contact Maria. When we were liberated by the Russians, we tried desperately to get in touch with her and tell her that we were safe. We were able to get through to her one time and we let her know that when we reached Berlin, we would try to make contact again. We again tried to reach Maria by phone, but without success. She still lived in her old apartment near the airport. Getting from place to place was a big problem. Transportation no longer existed, and neither Walter nor I was able to endure a six- to eight-

155

hour walk from our apartment on Oliverplatz to Heimstrasse 10, where Maria lived.

Our old friend Willi Melis came through for us once again. He had a bicycle, and we asked him if he would ride over to Maria's home, tell her where we were, and try to get her to come to see us. He did go, not once but a few times. Each time he met her, she refused to come, claiming that she did not want any thanks or recognition for what she had done to help us.

After some time, she finally relented, and with great effort made the long difficult trip to see us. We embraced, we kissed, we cried. This reunion was both happy and sad, but we were all grateful that it had taken place. Walter and I owed so much to this woman.

Chapter 24

Modest Maria

The war was over, and Willi and I were still trying to find food. I no longer had anything left to exchange for food. Life seemed impossible to bear.

One day, while I was sitting on the step of my apartment building, a friend of the Abrahams, Mr. Melis, approached me. He said the Abrahams had sent him to find me. They wanted to see me. Would I go with him to see them?

My first reaction was no, I didn't want to go. I thought to myself, Why should I go? I didn't want thanks for what I had done. To me, it was what had to be done – nothing special or unusual.

But after he had come to see me several times, I changed my mind. I took my children, and we somehow managed to get to where the Abrahams lived. Ruth was overjoyed that I had come and greeted me very warmly. She and Walter praised me for what I had done for them, and I was very happy to see them and little Reha again.

Ruth told me that she had had tuberculosis for some time. She now had to get treatment and would soon leave for Switzerland.

After Ruth and I caught up on the all the things that we had gone through during the war, she and Walter wanted to know what they could do for my family and me. I told them that my husband had no work. By then, Walter had made some connections with the

American Allies. He managed to get Willi a job as a driver for the American military. It was a good job, and he enjoyed working for them. He kept that job for twenty years.

Ruth and Walter also helped us get a more comfortable apartment on a low floor, so we moved from our apartment near the airport to Zehlendorf.

Ruth spent several months in Switzerland recovering from her illness. I knew that they had plans to leave Germany, and once she returned from Switzerland they would leave for the United States. Ruth and I had become very close. She was the friend I never had. We saw each other as often as possible, and we shared everything with each other, even the packages of food and clothing she received from her sisters in America and Scotland. It was very difficult for me when the Abrahams left Germany.

The Abrahams left in the spring of 1948, a few months before my daughter Renate was born. Once they were settled in America, they sent us packages of food. Every month, food arrived. These packages were a tremendous help to my entire family, and I will never forget this. My son Gerhard was very sick, so Ruth sent canned meat products and other nourishing food supplies for us. Ruth and Walter helped us, and I accepted this, even though I didn't want to at first. I had mixed feelings about it, but I accepted their help because I was in great need.

I missed Ruth and her family, I missed our deep friendship. But as time passed, even though she was far away, Ruth became more than a sister – she was like a mother to me.

Chapter 25

The Sweet Taste of Freedom

In Berlin, Walter and I found out that a small group of Jews, who had survived, had set up an organization to help themselves and others with food, shelter, and other basic needs. A few weeks later, they offered us a more comfortable furnished apartment nearby. This apartment had once housed the Spanish ambassador to Berlin. It was quite elegant. The rooms were very large, and we even had a view of a park across the street. The furnishings were very beautiful, but we were hardly able to appreciate this because of the constant hunger pangs we were enduring.

The food situation was desperate – not just for us but for everybody. Reha couldn't stop crying, "I am hungry! I am hungry!" Night and day, she cried so. Every morning we went down to the Jewish organization and waited in line for a card that would entitle us to a small amount of rations. One day, while we were standing there, with Reha crying, a woman turned to us. She had a small piece of white bread and handed it to Reha. As I thanked her, I recognized her as my cousin Frieda, the daughter of my father's brother, Uncle Marcus. We had both lived in Allenstein, many years before. It turned out that she, too, had hidden during the war, and she appeared to be the only survivor of her entire family. We made an effort to keep in touch with each other, but with communication being almost non-existent and Frieda not having any real address, this turned out to be an impossible task.

Before the war ended in the spring of 1945, the rest of the Allies began to converge on Berlin at that time, and we now heard that the British were arriving. With Reha, I started to go to where they were billeted in order to plead and beg for food. On the way, in front of the Café Leon, I came across a group of British soldiers. I told them how starved we were. They could hear little Reha crying only two words, "I'm hungry. I'm hungry." They must have been very good people because without a question, they gave me every bit of food and rations they were carrying. I was so grateful, I could only sob my thanks to them.

Another time, we heard that the American soldiers were going to be marching through Berlin. The arrival of the rest of the Allies gave us a feeling that is difficult to explain. More than the sight of the Russians coming in victoriously through the town in which we had lived, the arrival of the Americans brought forth joy and relief. Our hearts were filled to bursting with happiness. Now, with the arrival of all the Allies, some good would be coming to Berlin, something that we as Jews could at last look forward to. We had been liberated by the Russians in Neudamm, but we still endured great anxiety, sickness, and extreme hunger. I became ill. The cough that lingered was a symptom of the tuberculosis I had, for which I required many months of treatment. The Jewish organization in Berlin had not yet gotten their food program properly set up. We were still begging for daily nourishment, and we hoped that these deprivations would soon disappear. With the arrival of the British and the Americans, we felt that our long nightmare was finally coming to an end.

Walter wanted to go to see the American soldiers. They were going to march near Weissensee, a long way from where we lived, on the other side of town. He was still very weak, but he insisted and would not be deterred.

160

So, Walter would go for all of us. It was decided that he should wear a little blue and white badge to show the soldiers that he was Jewish. Now my sewing ability came to wonderful use. I found some scraps of material and put together a little badge to pin on his jacket. How strange! All these years being forced to wear the yellow star to identify us as Jews, and now we were proudly displaying the blue and white colors in Germany, announcing to one and all our pride in being Jewish.

It took Walter several hours of walking to get from our neighborhood to where the parade was being held. He finally reached a crowd of people who were lining the streets to welcome the American soldiers. It was not a huge crowd, but there were enough people who were sick of the Nazis – pacifists, Jews, news correspondents, Germans just worn out from war – to make a respectable turnout. The American soldiers rode down the streets in their tanks smiling, singing, and waving – victoriously. Walter stood there taking it all in. Miraculously, an American soldier, noticing the blue and white badge that Walter was wearing, broke ranks, rushed over, and embraced him.

They spoke for a very short time, but Walter was able to convey to the soldier that we were starving, that he had a wife and a young child at home with nothing to eat. The soldier ran his hands through his pockets, and took out what he had – a few bars of candy. To the American it was nothing, but to Walter it was like a treasure – chocolate candy bars, rich and sweet. How Reha would love them!

Then Walter reached into his pocket. I had written down Anna's address in Philadelphia and had given it to Walter before he left. Walter now took the crinkled little scrap of paper and handed it to the soldier.

"My wife's sister," he said. "Save it. And when you get back to America, find her. Please tell her that we are still alive."

He did.

161

Epilogue

The war was over, yet it took Walter, Reha, and me three years to leave Germany. I needed to recover from tuberculosis, and both Walter and I had to overcome our misgivings and fear of rebuilding our lives in a new, foreign land. In the end, we knew that we must.

We could no longer remain in Germany. We left in May 1948 for America and settled in New York City, where Walter and I found work – he delivering furniture, and me sewing dolls in a factory. Eventually, Walter was able to establish a furniture business, and I became – as always – his partner and helpmate.

Walter and I were fortunate; we were blessed with the birth of a son, John Mark in 1952. Both Reha and John are a source of pride and comfort to me and have, over the years, provided me with much joy in my grandchildren and great-grandchildren. My beloved Walter died in the fall of 1979.

My sisters Anna Aron, Edith Meyerhoff, and Betty Winograd are deceased. My mother-in-law, Elsa Strauss Abraham, survived the war. Her knowledge of French saved her from the gas chambers, and she immigrated to the United States a few years after we did. Elsa's parents, Ludwig and Clara Strauss, were interned in Gurs, France; they did not survive. Their heartbreaking letters from Gurs, pleading for help, describe the horrific conditions under which they lived. My father-in-law, Julius Abraham, perished in Majdanek in September 1943. My parents, Meyer and Frieda Fromm, were deported to Thereseinstadt, transport no. I30, in July 1942. From there they were sent to Treblinka, where they died in September 1942. My sister Ella Kessler, her husband Martin, and their children Helga and Johnny perished at Auschwitz in January 1943. My Aunt Marta Lewin, Uncle Sally, and their granddaughter Mara were transported to Auschwitz and perished.

Josef Müller, whom I met at Dachau in 1938, contacted me after the war. He sent me a beautiful gold enamel wristwatch. A few months later, I received a letter from someone who had worked for him, informing me that Josef Müller had committed suicide for fear of being tried for his work at Dachau. I was never able to find out exactly what he had done at that concentration camp, but it may have been through his intervention that Walter's father was released.

When the war ended, Walter and I went to the Goedes, but we were unable to locate them. We were told that they did not survive the war.

Gabriele Maas, whose path always seemed to cross mine at the worst of times, survived the war. She had tried to escape to Denmark but was captured and imprisoned by the Nazis for being a Communist and a half-Jew. During the liberation, she was sexually abused by the Russians. Several years later, she immigrated to England. Gabriele died many years ago.

My best friend, Jutta Salzmann Benton, was sent to England by her parents in the early 1930s, where she worked as a mother's helper. Jutta met her future husband there, and that is where she has remained to this day. Her parents were able to join her in England. She now lives in London, and we speak regularly.

My silver candlesticks – those that we gave to a German friend in Berlin for safekeeping – have a story of their own. The house that our friend lived in was bombed and completely destroyed. Miraculously, the candlesticks remained intact. Our friend retrieved them from the rubble that was once her house, and they were returned to us after the war. Reha uses those silver heirlooms every Shabbos and holiday.

No conclusion of my story could be complete without talking about Maria. Being able to celebrate her 90th birthday with her in Germany was a dream come true for my family and me.

In retrospect, I can think of so many little characteristics and events that best exemplify the essence of who she was.

Maria gave birth to a beautiful little girl named Renate on September 16, 1948. Sweet and giving, she was the sunshine of the Nickel family. In February 1956, Renate contracted German measles. At first, she appeared to recover; but then, infected with meningitis, Renate passed away. Maria lived in her own world of sorrow and desperation, yet she transcended this tragedy and went on.

Maria was a strict and loving mother, rising early in the morning to help Joachim deliver newspapers so he could earn enough money to buy a much-desired moped.

A poetic spirit stirred within Maria. Her children grew up hearing her recite lengthy verses of *Der Zauberlehrling* by Johann Wolfgang Goethe and *Das Lied von der Glocke* by Friedrich Schiller. Music and song were her passion. One time, she actually had a captive audience. In the early 1950s, while on an illegal shopping expedition for cheaper food in East Berlin, Maria was apprehended. She suddenly disappeared, no one knew what had happened to her. It took a few days for her family to find her. She had been sentenced by the East Berlin police to four weeks in prison. But true to her indomitable spirit, she sang for her fellow prisoners, filling them with joy and cheer.

Maria lost more loved ones: Willi, her husband, died in the summer of 1970; and her oldest son, Gerhard, died in April 1974. Life went on for Maria until January 21, 2001.

My story is being told in memory of Walter, my parents, all my loved ones, and Maria of blessed memory. It also bears witness to the dehumanizing effects of prejudice, racism, and hatred.

Yet, I still believe that the essence of goodness and kindness exists and is stronger than all the horror I have witnessed – as evidenced by our survival...

One might think that this is a beautiful ending for a pathetically sad and moving story.

It is.

But do not for a moment think that the relationships, the feelings, and the sense of family stopped at this point.

Our families kept in very close contact during the ensuing years. Weekly phone calls; my biannual visits to Germany; two visits to us in the United States by Maria; a tree planting event in Israel at Yad Vashem, recognizing Maria as one of the Righteous Among the Nations attended not only by Maria, but also by Walter, Reha, my granddaughter, Ellana, and me. The ceremony at Yad Vashem was solemn, moving and memorable.

The marriages of our children, the births of our grandchildren, and great grandchildren, and the loss of our respective spouses as mentioned above. All, have kept us together.

Reha Sums Up

It's Sunday, May 21, 2000, the day before the birthday celebration, and everything has gone smoothly so far. It was no small feat to get nine people to a foreign country at a specific time without lost luggage, long delays, or missed flights. Arranging for eighty kosher meals that were brought along with us, as well as hotel rooms, transportation and, above all, the birthday dinner party at the Berlin Jewish Community House took the organizational and methodical skills of a senior chief of staff – my husband, Al.

Today we are together with Maria, and her son, Joachim – Joachim, my first and only childhood friend. We blend together as one family. I look at my mother, Ruth, and sense her tension at returning to Berlin, at facing again the memories of the life she once had there together with my father. She often tells me that she couldn't have made it without him, without his strength, his support, and his sense of humor. I look at Maria, dazzled at being among so many people, not truly believing that she, this shy, lonely, self-effacing woman, has become the center of so much attention.

The newspapers in Germany, sensing a story that their readers would appreciate, send reporters to interview Maria and my mother. Barbara Sofer, a writer based in Israel, is sent by *Woman's Day* magazine to write the story of Ruth and Maria.

I think they inhibit Maria and make her feel somewhat nervous. She whispers to me, "Since I haven't had so much schooling, I have never really felt comfortable with smart, educated people like these." They interview Maria, and among the many questions is the one that is always asked, "What made you do it?" And the response is always the same: "I hated what was being done to the Jews, I hated what was happening to Germany. How could I not?"

After the interviews, we return to the place where it all began, Willibald-Alexis-Strasse. My mother and Maria, two indomitable forces, walking arm-in-arm, reminisce and point to the building that had once housed the pharmaceutical factory, from where they had thwarted Hitler sixty years ago. Everything – the people on the street, the building, the shops – all look so ordinary, so banal. It's difficult to believe that here, on this street, a Jewish family was saved by the kindness of one stranger reaching out to another.

The day of Maria's birthday, Monday, May 22, is upon us, a celebration of ninety years of life with close family and friends. She is surprised when shortly before the party, we present her with a poster board collage of photographs: Maria as a young woman; Maria's parents; Maria and Willi; Maria and her children; Maria with my parents; and Maria planting her carob tree at Yad Vashem.

My family and I are the first to arrive. My husband Al had insisted upon getting there early to guarantee that everything was the way he had ordered. My daughter Ellana, her husband Efraim and their two children; my brother John and his daughter, Danielle; and, of course, my mother together make up our family group.

At 6 p.m. our guests begin to arrive at the Jewish Community House. The dining room is filled with colorful birthday balloons and bouquets of flowers. My two little granddaughters, Nicole and Eden, walk around, arranging flowers and spreading colorful sparkles all over the tables. Soon after, Maria, escorted by her son, Joachim, his wife Marlis, and her mother, appear. Other close family members arrive: Doris, Maria's late son Gerhard's widow, and her two sons, Egbert and Stefan. Yad Vashem representative Stephen Kramer and Israel Consulate press attaché Yuval Fuchs, along with Rabbi Techtal and Rabbi Ehrenberg, with the cantor of his congregation, are among our honored guests.

The food is delicious, and the mood festive and joyous. My mother, who had worried about putting all this together from afar, is thrilled to see her dream become a reality. Maria, so very anxious not to make an error or forget anything, stands up and without even waiting to be properly introduced, or for everyone to be seated, starts reading her speech, which she had worked on for many days. As she was, so was her speech. Soft and to the point, declining any suggestion of bravery and being eternally grateful for the show of love that permeated the room. There are more speeches, but as we approach the end of the dinner, the cantor stands up and in a glorious voice begins to sing a few Jewish songs. Our guests are enraptured and begin to clap their hands and hum along. Many of those present had never heard a cantor sing before, let alone Jewish songs. And many had never really heard the whole story of Maria and Ruth. Now they had heard it and now they knew!

* * * * *

Nine months after Maria's party, on January 21, 2001, Maria Nickel Rimkus, while on her way to church, collapsed on a street in Berlin close to where she lived. She was taken to a hospital, but she never regained consciousness. She died one hour later. My mother and I were devastated: we had lost our dearest friend. We both flew to Berlin to comfort Joachim, to attend Maria's funeral, and to pay our heartfelt respect to the woman who loved us and whom we loved.

Barbara Sofer, the writer who had joined us in Berlin two years earlier, to interview Maria for *Woman's Day* magazine, shared our grief and decided to feature Maria's heroism in her weekly column in *The Jerusalem Post*. She began by writing, "An angel died last week." She concluded by saying, "Bookstores carry whole sections on angels these days. The kind of angel I believe in is Maria Nickel – who proved that inside each one of us is the potential to serve as one of God's holy messengers." Barbara was unable to attend Maria's funeral; instead of going to Berlin, she wrote, "I'll visit her carob tree in Yad Vashem. There, among the Righteous of The Nations, she will always be of blessed, blessed memory."

Al and I have also visited Maria's carob tree, which stands on a windy, lonely hilltop. She had traveled to Jerusalem and planted it as a sapling many years ago. Over 18,000 such trees for as many heroes have been planted in the promenade known as the Avenue of The Righteous Among the Nations.

Why a carob tree? Because it is an evergreen that blooms all year round; it is a fruit-bearing tree; and it is not a very tall tree. It characterizes the Righteous. It exemplifies Maria. She was as steadfast and constant as the tree she planted; she was as giving and sustaining as its fruit; and as selfless and modest as its stature. May her memory be a blessing for us all.

Vermögenserklärung

Vornamen (Rufname unterstreichen) und Zuname (bei Ehefrauen auch Mädchenname):

Meyer Israel Fromm

Beruf: *ohne*   Jude? *ja*

Letzte Beschäftigung (Firma, Gehalt, Lohn):

Wohnung (Stadt, Stadtteil, Straße und Hausnummer, seit wann?

Berlin Wilmersdorf, Duisburgerstr. 1, seit März 1942

Name, Anschrift und evtl. jüdische Rassezugehörigkeit des Hauseigentümers:

unbekannt, da Untermieter

Größe der Wohnung (Zimmerzahl und -art, WC, Warmwasser, Dampf- oder Warmwasserheizung, Balkon, Wohngeschoß, Fahrstuhl, Gartenbenutzung, Nebenräume wie Diele, Badezimmer, Mädchenkammer, Keller, Boden usw. Genaue Angaben):

1 Durchgangszimmer

Höhe der monatlichen oder vierteljährlichen usw. Miete (Mietvertrag beifügen):

monatl. M.60.- à 15.- Anteil für Licht u. Licht

Sind Sie Untermieter? (Dann auch Name, Anschrift und evtl. jüdische Rassezugehörigkeit des Untervermieters angeben):

Ja

Hauptmieterin: Elsa Sara Herzog, Duisburgerstr. 1.

jüdin

Evaluation of residence of Meyer Fromm (Ruth's father) and its valuables. This document was distributed to the Jews either at their homes or at the deportation center.

171

2:

Seite 1

Wohnungsliste Aktenzeichen OFP 11379

Berlin- Duisburger Straße: _____ Nr. 1 Lage: V.I

Früherer Mieter bzw. Untermieter: _____ Meyer Israel Fromm b/Herzog
(Früherer Eigentümer der Gegenstände) Mittelzimmer

Inventory + Appraisel
Inventar und Bewertung

Blattnummer der Schätzung	Stück	Gegenstand	Nähere Kennzeichnung	Bewertung in RM Möbel und Hausrat	Textilien	Bemerkungen über Aufarbeitung usw.
	1	Kleiderschrank	Nussbaum	250,-		
	2	Wäscheschranke	dto.			
	1	Kleiderschrank	Lackiert	25,-		
	1	dto.	Mahagoni	20,-		
	1	Metallbettstelle m.Auflg.				
	1	dto. ohne "		20,-		
	1	Nähtisch 90 cm		35,-		
	1	Lehnstuhl		60,-		
	1	Eckschrank		2,-		
	1	5-fl.Krone		10,-		
	3	Stühle		8,-		
	1	kl.Tisch		1,-		
	1	Koffer		10,-		
	1	Reisekorb m.Küchengerät		5,-		
	1	Bild im Goldrahmen		10,-		
	1	Übergardine				
	2	Steppdecken				
	2	Federbetten				
	1	Frackanzug	---			
	5	Hose u. 1 Weste				
	1	Bademantel, 2 Frauenkleider, Posten Wäsche			40,-	
				560	40	

Inventory and appraisal of total contents of the residence of Meyer Fromm

IV. Wohnungsinventar und Kleidungsstücke (Anzahl und Wertangaben):

1. **Möbel und Einrichtungsgegenstände:**

a) S c h l a f z i m m e r :

	RM.		*RM.*		*RM.*		*RM.*
Kleiderschrank		Sofa — Couch		Kopfkissen		Nachttischlampen	
Bettstellen		Sessel		Unterbetten		Stehlampe	
Nachttische		Teppich		Daunenbetten		Frisiergarnitur	
Stühle		Bettvorleger		Steppdecken		Waschtischgarnitur	
Frisiertoilette		Brücken		Plumeaux		Wäschetruhe	
Waschtisch		Gardinen, Stores		Matratzen		*1 Tisch*	
Kommode		Federbetten		Deckenlampe			

b) W o h n -, H e r r e n z i m m e r :

Schreibtisch und Sessel		Krone — Lampe		Schreibtischuhr		Bücher
		Schreibtischlampe		Schreibplatte		Lexikon
Bücherschrank		Stehlampe		Schreibmaschine		Weltgeschichte
Bücherregale		Wandleuchter		Papierkorb		Prachtbände
Tisch, groß		Stand-Wand-Uhr		Gardinen, Stores		Atlanten
Tisch, klein		Spiegel				Globus
Stühle		Teppich				
Sofa — Couch		Brücken				
Sessel		Schreibgarnitur				

c) S p e i s e z i m m e r :

Eßtisch		Anrichte		Steh-, Wandlampe		Hausbar
Stühle		Vitrine		Teppich		Gardinen, Stores
Sessel		Sofa — Couch		Brücken		
Buffet		Krone, Lampe		Teewagen		

d) D i e l e , B a d e z i m m e r :

Dielengarnitur		Lampe		Schrank, klein	
Flurgarderobe		Spiegel			
Läufer		Schrank, groß		Vorleger	

e) K ü c h e , K a m m e r :

Küchenschrank		Kohlenkasten		Küchengeschirr zusammen		Vorräte, eingeweckt
Anrichte		Lampe		Gardinen		Vorräte, weitere
Besenschrank		Waage		Kühlschrank		
Küchentisch		Kochtöpfe usw.		eig. Gas-, Elektro-Herd		
Küchenstühle				Bügeleisen		
Leiter						

f) K i n d e r -, F r e m d e n z i m m e r , S a l o n :

Inventory of total contents of the residence of Meyer Fromm

g) Balkon, Wintergarten, Keller, Boden:

kg Kohle			kg Kartoffeln		
kg Koks					
kg Holz					

h) Verschiedenes:

Klavier, Flügel	Rauchtisch	Theaterglas		
Geige	Nähtisch	Reisekoffer	Werkzeug	
	Nähmaschine			
Radioapparat	Staubsauger	Hunde		
Plattenspieler	Höhensonne			
Plattenschrank	Föhn	Fahrrad		
Schallplatten	Kino-, Foto-	Motorrad		
Noten	Apparat	Kraftwagen		

2. Tafelgeschirr, Bestecke, Kristall:

Speiseservice		Tafelgerät Silber		
Teile	*Grosses Geschirr*	Tafelgerät Silber		
Kaffeeservice		Tafelgerät Silber	Kristall	
Teile	Besteckkasten			
Stck.	mit ...... Teilen			
Gläser	Silber, Alpaka			
Stck.	Tafelgerät Silber			
Geschirr				

3. Wäsche:

Tischdecken		Küchentücher	Wolldecken	
Servietten	*Grosse Wäsche*		Plüschdecken	
Kaffeedecken				
Servietten	Badelaken			
Garn. Bettwäsche	Frottiertücher	Kissen		
	Handtücher	Decken		

4. Kleidungsstücke:
   a) Herrenkleidung: *evens*

1. Frack			Kragen	
Smoking	-Uniform	3 Oberhemden	Paar Strümpfe	
Gehrock, Cut	Uniform-Mantel	Schlafanzüge	Paar Handschuhe	
Straßenanzüge	Uniform-Mütze	Hausjacke	Schals	
Wintermäntel	Ausrüstungsstücke	Garnituren Unterwäsche		
Uebergangsmäntel	Skianzug			
Sommermäntel	Paar Skistiefel	Krawatten		
Pelzmäntel	Pullover	Paar Schuhe, Stiefel		
	Sportkleidung			
Herrenhüte				

Inventory of total contents of the residence of Meyer Fromm

Transport list of German Jews sent to concentration camps. Meyer and Frieda Fromm, Reha's grandparents, appear as numbers 60 and 61 on the list.

Geburtsurkunde

(Standesamt Berlin -Wilmersdorf--- Nr. 357/1943)

Reha A b r a h a m---

ist am 19. Januar 1943 um 9 Uhr 30 Minuten---

in Berlin -Wilmersdorf, Paulsborner Straße 7 geboren.

Vater: Arbeiter Walter Wilhelm Israel ---
A b r a h a m, mosaisch---

Mutter: Arbeiterin Ruth Sara A b r a h a m, geborene
F r o m m, mosaisch, beide wohnhaft in Berlin-
Wilmersdorf.---

Änderungen der Eintragung: _____

Berlin -Schmargendorf---, den 22. Januar--- 19 43

Der Standesbeamte
In Vertretung:

-,30RM Gebühren bezahlt.   Sch.

Stand A 27
Mat. 2843 ● Din A 5. 60000. 5. 42 BU

Reha's Birth Certificate issued on January 22, 1943

176